ABRAHAM
'WOLE HAASTRUP

# THE 3RD EPISTLE

A LEADERSHIP REMINISCENCE

# THE THIRD EPISTLE
(A Leadership Reminiscence)

Global Kingdom Influence (GKI)
Coburg, Vic. 3058, Australia.

HOUSE OF ISRAEL
PUBLISHING COMPANY

The Third Epistle (A Leadership Reminiscence) Copyright @ 2021 by Abraham 'Wole Haastrup

All rights reserved. No part of this book may be produced, stored in a retrieval system, or transmitted in any form or by any means – electronic, mechanical, photocopy, recording, scanning, or any other – except for brief quotations in printed reviews, without the permission of the publisher.

Global Kingdom Influence (GKI)
(Biblical Truth, Leadership, & Christian Advocacy) Coburg North, Vic 3058, Australia.
ISBN 978–0–992-3823-7-7

Unless otherwise indicated, Scripture quotations are from The New King James Version of the Holy Bible, copyright 1982 – Thomas Nelson, Inc. used by permission.

Printed in Nigeria - **House of Israel Publishing Company**
Plot 3, Block 4, Estate 12, RCCG. Redemption Camp, Ogun State, Nigeria.
Plot3, Omoniyi Estate, Off Benin/Owo Expressway, Akure, Ondo State, Nigeria. Tel: +234-8034082781, +234-8096588871.
e-mail: houseofisreal2020@gmail.com

# TABLE OF CONTENTS

| | |
|---|---|
| Preface | vii |
| Introduction | x |

## 1    Leadership In Context    13

| | |
|---|---|
| 1.1 Leadership In Context | 15 |
| 1.2 The Bane of Leadership - I | 23 |
| 1.3 The Bane of Leadership - II | 35 |
| 1.4 The Bane of Leadership – III | 41 |
| 1.5 Lost Sheep & the Lost Shepherd | 49 |
| 1.6 A Little Leaven | 57 |

## 2.    Leadership & Succession    63

| | |
|---|---|
| 2.1 Succession- God's Own Idea | 65 |
| 2.2 Leadership & Succession | 69 |
| 2.3 Leadership Transition | 79 |
| 2.4 Joshua – A Leadership Post-Mortem | 89 |
| 2.5 Where Are The Jethro Fathers? | 93 |

| | | |
|---|---|---|
| **3.** | **Building To Last** | **98** |

| | |
|---|---|
| 3.1 Building To Last | 99 |
| 3.2 Joshua - A Leadership Post-Mortem | 103 |
| 3.3 The Sons of Eli | 107 |
| 3.4 In The Days of Samuel | 117 |
| 3.5 Catching The Spirit of the Leader (Finishing Well) | 129 |
| | |
| Acknowledgements | 133 |
| Appendices | 135 |
| Notes | 136 |
| For Further Readings | 138 |

**The Challenge of Spiritual Leadership:**

*"Spiritual leaders should not only seek to make those they lead better, BUT to also be the best they ought to be - spiritually, and in all other areas of life. Otherwise, the many things the followers don't know will continue to limit them!"*

.(Anonymous)

# Preface

The word 'Epistle' was used in not less than three contexts in the New Testament of the Holy Bible.

Twice, Apostle Paul used it. In II Corinthians 3:2-3, he wrote:
> *"You are our epistle written in our hearts, known and read by all men; clearly you are an epistle of Christ, ministered by us, written not with ink but by the Spirit of the living God, not on tablets of stone but on tablets of flesh, that is, of the heart."*

Here, Apostle Paul implies that the converts God helped him to make in his several mission trips were evidences that he had not labored in vain. They were written as memorials in his heart as well as in the heart of those who laboured with him. These Converts were also an epistle of Christ that men could read. He therefore urged them to live right so that even when the people who could not read or have access to the Bible came across them as epistles, they would see Jesus.

Also, Apostle Paul called his personal letters to the churches 'my Epistles', and he commanded that the letters be read to all churches in each of the cities to which he sent them (Colossians 4:16; I Thessalonians 5:27).

Furthermore, several Books of the New Testament besides the four Gospels, and The Acts of the Apostles were generally called 'Epistle'. They were credited to the individuals whom God used to write them. These 'Epistles' were also addressed to the churches in cities, as well as people in different situations. Many of the Epistles dealt with issues that ranged from doctrines, and discipleship, to Christian Service, as well as church leadership, etc.

In summary, an Epistle is an open letter - a message on paper from one person - especially a leader, to another. Such messages often convey the leader's heart, and are meant to positively influence or impact the reader's life. The Epistles found in the Bible were a very vital part of the post- Resurrection missionary activities of the Apostles of the Early Church. Through the Epistles, the writers - from Peter, Paul, to John the Beloved, etc, -

wrote to instruct the new and emerging congregations on the importance of their newfound life, and how to live it out.

In addition to encouraging the new Christians, the Epistles equally aimed at putting in place administrative structures that would help leadership and succession in the churches.

When the Lord dropped "The Third Epistle" in my heart as the title for this book, I began to ponder on the relevance to the issues of leadership and succession.

Essentially, the known Epistles in the Bible had a dual purpose:
- First, they were writings and admonitions to the emerging Christians who were just being reached with the light of the Gospel of Jesus (Romans 1:16-17). The purpose as explained above, was to show them how to live out the new life.
- Second, these same Epistles also prescribed guidelines on Church administration.

    This book; *"The Third Epistle (A Leadership Reminiscence)"*, is a focus on leaders – who they are (or ought to be), how they lead (or ought to lead), and What legacy they should aim at leaving behind as they move out of the scene – either by age, death, or, as God may have it, by Rapture.

# Introduction

This book - *"The Third Epistle (A Leadership Reminiscence)* is on Biblical Leadership & Succession. It gleans leadership issues and characters across both the Old and New Testaments of the Bible. The persons, lives and performances of leaders across the Bible are therefore the raw materials for this book.

In particular, the book focuses on the strengths, weaknesses and styles of leaders. It then drew lessons from the internal, external and/or environmental factors that helped or hindered the fulfilments of purpose and destinies of these leaders. The whole objective is to help leaders and aspiring leaders of today – secular, and especially spiritual, learn one or two things so they too can avoid the pitfalls of those who had gone before. This book is not on the theory of Leadership per se. Rather, it is on it's practice. It looks at what the Bible said and revealed about the subject of Leadership and Succession. It also brings to the fore, what I believe the Holy Spirit made clear to me from the Scriptures over the years, as God groomed me while I served under various leaders. Conceptual issues and leadership theories are mentioned in a few places in the book only where they would help the grasping of what was being discussed.

The book is divided into three parts. Centred around the sub-theme 'Leadership In Context', Part 1 is essentially an overview on the subject of Leadership and Succession. This section also looked at some 'Banes' of Leadership. In Part 2 we focused on some spiritual issues in leadership and Succession. Here, some of the ingredients of excellent leadership are enumerated. Finally, in Part 3 of the book, we considered the crucial place of 'building to last'. This part also looked at a few of what had seduced and derailed some leaders in history. It is believed that since God has not changed (and will never change), leaders today and those who aspire to lead will surely gain some insights and avoid same pitfalls.

As you go through, may the Holy Spirit make your heart receptive, so that the word of God can come *to* you, and *for* you. Peradventure some leaders come to your mind as you ponder on the subjects in this book, ask the Holy Spirit to tell you what you can do to help them.

I pray too that as we all aspire to be the Salt of the earth and the Light of the world, may we never lose our own salt and light in Jesus Name (I Corinthians 9:27). Happy reading.

# LEADERSHIP IN CONTEXT

# LEADERSHIP IN CONTEXT

**1.1** Leadership In Context

**1.2** The Bane of Leadership - I

**1.3** The Bane of Leadership - II

**1.4** The Bane of Leadership – III

**1.5** Lost Sheep & the Lost Shepherd

**1.6** A Little Leaven

# LEADERSHIP IN CONTEXT
*(An Overview)*

Leadership is a wide subject. Leadership has both physical and spiritual dimensions.

Of course, spiritual leadership is more important and more critical than physical or secular leadership.

Many things happen under spiritual leadership that are not allowed or tolerated in secular leadership. For example, spiritual leaders can oppress or exploit their followers and get away with it (at least in the physical). In the same way, followers and subordinates of spiritual leaders can rebel or insult the leader. Such followers can even use and abuse the leader's name, and also get away with it (again at least to a large extent). The good and comforting fact is that there is a God who is no respecter of persons (Acts 10:34-35)! That God is also the One who will do the final marking. He is all-seeing and all-knowing (I Sam 16:7; Matt 6:4,6). In Psalm 139: 11-12, the Psalmist said:

> *"If I say, "Surely the darkness shall fall on me," Even the night shall be light about me; Indeed, the darkness shall not hide from You, But the night shines as the day; The darkness and the light are both alike to You."*

In this Opening chapter, we shall take an overview of some issues in context, as we ask the following Questions:
+ What is spiritual Leadership?
+ Why do we need spiritual leaders and spiritual leadership?
+ Who is a spiritual leader?
+ How can we become <u>effective</u> (and <u>right</u>) spiritual leaders?

Also, we will be considering the importance of Succession. We'll conclude with a look at some examples of biblical leadership and succession.

## What is spiritual Leadership (Christian Leadership)?

Spiritual (Christian) Leadership is the act of <u>influencing, and serving others</u> out of Christ's interests in their lives so they can accomplish God's purposes for and through them," - that's according to Bill Lawrence[1] (president of Leader Formation International, at Bible.org.)

Christian or spiritual leadership is not rooted in worldly notions of success, such as the love of money or power. Jesus Himself spoke against this when expressing the importance of serving others.

Spiritual or Christian Leadership concerns all and everything that have to do with two things: Leadership from spiritual or Christian perspective; and/or leading Christian or spiritual organizations.
While spiritual leadership involves many of the same principles as general leadership, spiritual leadership has certain distinctive qualities that must be understood and practiced if spiritual or Christian leaders are to be successful (Matthew 20:25-28).

**Why do we need spiritual leaders and spiritual leadership?**
God is a God of purpose, goals & plans. He has a Kingdom purpose and plan for the entire universe and in particular for men and generations. In His infinite wisdom, God has tied the fulfilment of His grand plan to, and has put everything under His Son, Jesus Christ (Ephesians 1:10-11).

Primary or central to God's purpose is the redemption of man. It is important to recognize that God gives men opportunities to be involved in the achievement of His purpose. Not only this, HE even allocates special roles to man, including leadership roles.

**Why does God choose leaders?**
In different dispensations, God chooses leaders because He often needed an anchor man - someone He could give instructions to, and who He also could hold accountable. For example, in Bible times, He chose people like Moses, Eli, Saul, David, Solomon, the Apostles, particularly someone like Paul, etc.

A leader is critical in any setting. The role of the leader in impacting or influencing his or her followers cannot be overemphasized. It continued to be said that "everything rises and falls with the leader".

**The Leader God chooses:**
- Wherever there is crisis, God always sends the solution through highly capable and transformed Leaders. Hence, it is said that:
- Nothing happens without leadership,
- Nothing changes without leadership,
- Nothing develops without leadership,
- Nothing improves without leadership, and of course,
- Nothing is corrected without leadership.

Perhaps it can be said right away that since there is no leader without a follower, it is good not to forget that followers too can play a major role in the success or failure of leaders. Followers like Joshua, Elisha, Timothy, Gehazi, Judas, Demas, etc, no doubt had their places in history.

Foundation for Spiritual leadership:
Leading is not a position, it is not in a title, It is not by inheritance. It is never demanded, it is earned. Leadership is finding your gift and serving it to others. That is why it is relatively easy to know or recognize a good or true leader. A true leader influences others to do what is right in God's sight. He or she works to see people carry out the perfect and acceptable will of God. In other words, leaders bring people into a Win-Win situation. They win and help their followers to win, and by so doing, the organization (in our case, the Kingdom of God), also wins.
There are qualifications for true spiritual leadership. These include
+ character,
+ spiritual maturity,
+ faith (both as a fruit, and also, as a gift of the Holy Spirit).

The Spiritual Leader has a lot of work on his or her hands.
It takes a leader to move an organization forward. Somebody said 'You cannot build a Giant organization with a Pygmy leader'.

In Matthew 20:25-26, our Lord Jesus Christ said there are two kingdoms (and in essence), two kinds of leaders: - worldly leaders & Kingdom (transformed) leaders. He went on to say that Worldly leaders lord it over their people while kingdom leaders are called to serve their followers. This means that Kingdom leaders are servant leaders.

In His wisdom, God made some leaders unique – unique in their giftings and accomplishments. While there are unique leaders, however, no leader is indispensable!

It is to be noted too that different Leaders have different assignment(s) or focus which God gives to them.

For Moses, the main mandate was:
*"Come now therefore, And I will send thee unto Pharaoh, that thou mayest bring forth my people the children of Israel out of Egypt"* **(Exodus 3:10).**

To Joshua, God said:
> *"Moses my servant is dead; now therefore arise, go over this Jordan, thou, and all this people, unto the land which I do give to them, even to the children of Israel... Be strong and of a good courage: for unto this people shalt thou divide for an inheritance the land,*

*which I sware unto their fathers to give them."*
**(Joshua 1:2,6).**

**How can we become effective spiritual leaders?**
To be an effective spiritual leader, one needs first to know what effective spiritual leadership entails. An effective spiritual leader is the Leader who is <u>result-oriented</u> and who at the same time pleases the Master)?

Note: True effectiveness implies leading according to the mind and dictates of the Master, and doing so only for His glory (Jeremiah 48:10; Matthew 7:21-23; II Corinthians 4:1-3; II Corinthians 8:20-21).

Some lessons from the charge to Joshua (Joshua 1: 1-10):

* "be strong and very courageous so that thou mayest observe to do according to all the law which Moses my Servant commanded thee" He was to:

- Enforce the existing righteous ordinances/Biblical doctrines/standards and policies started by Moses;

- live by example;

- lead the people to battles (prayers/spiritual warfare, aggressive evangelism and Missions, church planting and growth, etc);

- come against/be ruthless with kings who dared oppose their entry into The Promised land (those who don't want positive changes and righteous standards.

- be focused - not be distracted or be derailed!

- learn from those who went before him - their strengths and weaknesses;

- look unto God - trust Him for help and for rewards (Psalm 37:1-5; Proverbs 3: 5-7)

- Keep Heaven in view (Luke 10:17-20; Acts 24:16; I Corinthians 9:27; II Corinthians 8:20-21; II Timothy 4:6-8).

We, and all emerging leaders are to do all these, and even more, if we too want to succeed in our own generation.

# THE BANE OF LEADERSHIP I

In this Chapter and the next two, we will be considering a very crucial subject as far as leadership and succession is concerned. That crucial subject is the bane of leadership. In all, five areas will be examined. In this Chapter, two of the banes are looked at. The rest are discussed in the subsequent chapters.

For our purpose in this book, we will define the word 'Bane' as a killer, or a poison that brings death and destruction. The word 'poison' itself, is said to be a substance that usually kills or injures through its chemical action.

The Bane of leadership is therefore that which seduces a leader, and brings him or her down. Not only does it have power to discredit a leader's testimony, it can prevent a leader from finishing well. It can also destroy a good legacy.

**Hypocrisy:**
In II Samuel 12:6-15, we read:
> *"Then David sent to Joab, saying, "Send me Uriah the Hittite." And Joab sent Uriah to David. When Uriah had come to him, David asked how Joab was doing, and how the people were doing, and how the war prospered. And David said to Uriah, "Go down to your house and wash your feet." So Uriah departed from the king's house, and a gift of food from the king followed him. But Uriah slept at the door of the king's house with all the servants of his lord, and did not go down to his house. So when they told David, saying, "Uriah did not go down to his house," David said to Uriah, "Did you not come from a journey? Why did you not go down to your house?" And Uriah said to David, "The ark and Israel and Judah are dwelling in tents, and my lord Joab and the servants of my lord are encamped in the open fields. Shall I then go to my house to eat and drink, and to lie with my wife? As you live, and as your soul lives, I will not do this thing." Then David said to Uriah, "Wait here today also, and tomorrow I will let you depart." So Uriah remained in Jerusalem that day and the next. Now*

*when David called him, he ate and drank before him; and he made him drunk. And at evening he went out to lie on his bed with the servants of his lord, but he did not go down to his house.*

*In the morning it happened that David wrote a letter to Joab and sent it by the hand of Uriah. And he wrote in the letter, saying, "Set Uriah in the fore front of the hottest battle, and retreat from him, that he may be struck down and die."*

In this passage, we read about how King David master-minded the untimely death of Uriah the Hittite – a loving husband, as well as a loyal and devoted soldier in the service of what we can liken to today's Israeli Defence Force (IDF). The loyalty and faithfulness of Uriah- both to Israel as a Nation, David her king, and above all to God - Israel's ultimate King, was unparalleled!

When asked by king David to go to his house and have a 'good' time with his family, Uriah exclaimed in II Samuel 11:11-13:
"And Uriah said to David, "The ark and Israel and Judah are dwelling in tents, and my lord Joab and the servants of my lord are encamped in the open fields. Shall I then go to my house to eat and drink, and to lie with my wife? As you live, and as your soul lives, I will not do this thing. "Then David said to Uriah, "Wait here today also, and tomorrow I will let you depart." So

Uriah remained in Jerusalem that day and the next. Now when David called him, he ate and drank before him; and he made him drunk. And at evening he went out to lie on his bed with the servants of his lord, but he did not go down to his house. "At the base of King David's undue generosity to an obscure but gallant soldier is a pure but disguised hypocrisy! David the king had a onetime extra-marital affair with Bathsheba, Uriah's wife. She sent the news that she was pregnant, she probably thought it a great honour to carry the king's royal seed. However, for king David, the thought of a cover up was uppermost in his mind. Hence, he asked General Joab to send Uriah home briefly. Meanwhile, palace officials - old and young would have been eavesdropping what the king did with one of his soldiers' wife. It's not unlikely too that at the morning and evening devotions, king David would still play the Harp, lead praise worship, and admonished from the Torah. A great confusion would have been on the faces of everyone. Questions on their minds may have included:

+ Has the God of Israel changed?
+ When it comes to sin, does He operate one standard for kings, and another for peasants? (Acts 10:34-35).
+ Doesn't God frown any more at sin, especially the sin of adultery?
+ Are wives of soldiers on National posting safe any more?

What a serious misrepresentation of Yahweh! Hence God sent a

Prophet named Nathan to confront the king about his grievous sins of adultery and murder.

Today, hypocrisy is still one of the major banes of Leadership. Many a leader pretend they love and care, to whatever extent they can, but the raw truth is that they may not be as caring and fatherly as they appear to be.

One of the ways hypocrisy as a bane of leadership has been playing out is that when some leaders smile at you or commend you, you must be quick to ask the Holy Spirit for the true meaning of their smiles! Many a time, I have seen people smile at me, and even praised me, rarely did I know that it was a 'valedictory' gesture. This is because to them, my matter had been sealed for evil. Oh how great, gracious and faithful our God is! On one very critical occasion, God went ahead to reverse the irreversible (Psalm 89:1, 22-24; Lam 3:37; Revelation 3: 7-8; Psalm 48:8-14).

**Seduction:**
The word 'Seduction' has been defined, among other things, as the act of seducing, or something that seduces, attracts, and charms. It is also said to be the enticement of a person to sexual intercourse.

It is important to point out that except in a special reference to King Solomon, the subject of seduction is being discussed in this book, only in the context of leadership and succession.

To seduce is to persuade to disobedience and disloyalty. To seduce is also to lead astray usually by persuasions or false promises. To seduce is to bewitch, to charm, to ensnare and to entrap.

A seducer is the person or thing that seduces. Two other words that will make things clearer to us here, are: 'bewitch', and 'charm'.

The word 'bewitch' means to influence or affect especially, injuriously by witchcraft. To charm, on the other hand, means to affect by or as if by magic.

Many things can seduce a leader. These include position, power, wealth, success, and of course, the opposite sex. King Solomon, as a leader was seduced on all sides, and by virtually everything. His God-given wisdom seduced him. Position, success, wealth, etc, all seduced him. And, of course, women seduced him.

There is a general saying that 'power corrupts, and absolute power corrupts absolutely'. Perhaps, this is more true in spiritual matters than it is in the physical. Many a spiritual leader have been seduced by God's gifts and graces upon their lives, especially the anointing. This leads us to two very important issues on our subject matter:

- How does seduction work, or put in another way, what fuels seduction?
- Also, what are some of the grave consequences of seduction?

A close look at the life and statements of Solomon will give us some clue: In 1 Kings 11:1-10; Ecclesiastics 2:10-12, we read:

> *"But King Solomon loved many foreign women, as well as the daughter of Pharaoh: women of the Moabites, Ammonites, Edomites, Sidonians, and Hittites—² from the nations of whom the LORD had said to the children of Israel, "You shall not intermarry with them, nor they with you. Surely they will turn away your hearts after their gods." Solomon clung to these in love. ³ And he had seven hundred wives, princesses, and three hundred concubines; and his wives turned away his heart. ⁴ For it was so, when Solomon was old, that his wives turned his heart after other gods; and his heart was not loyal to the LORD his God, as was the heart of his father David. For Solomon went after Ashtoreth the goddess of the Sidonians, and after Milcom the abomination of theAmmonites.*

*⁶ Solomon did evil in the sight of theLORD, and did not fully follow the LORD, as did his father David. ⁷ Then Solomon built a high place for Chemosh the abomination of Moab, on the hill that is east of Jerusalem, and for Molech the abomination of the people of Ammon. ⁸ And he did likewise for all his foreign wives, who burned incense and sacrificed to their gods.*

*⁹ So the LORD became angry with Solomon, because his heart had turned from the LORD God of Israel, who had appeared to him twice, ¹⁰ and had commanded him concerning this thing, that he should not go after other gods; but he did not keep what the LORD had commanded. ¹¹ Therefore the LORD said to Solomon, "Because you have done this, and have not kept My covenant and My statutes, which I have commanded you, I will surely tear the kingdom away from you and give it to your servant".*

*"¹⁰ Whatever my eyes desired I did not keep from them. I did not withhold my heart from any pleasure, For my heart rejoiced in all my labor; And this was my reward from all my labor.¹¹ Then I looked on all the works that my hands had done. And on the labor in which I had toiled; And indeed all was vanity and grasping for the wind. There was no profit under the sun."*

Several things can fuel seduction. For instance, self indulgence and lack of self control. Also, a self-deception that one is strong and in charge, as well as flattery by those who, though strategically placed around or near a leader, would rather praise or be quiet about his observed weaknesses and or excesses. In many cases, some leaders also build a wall around themselves that makes it difficult for those who should help them to reach them. This may be by being punitive with anyone who dared challenge their actions or their excesses. By surrounding themselves with sycophants, many a leader also dug their own grave! This is examined more closely in the next chapter. On Solomon, the above passage told us that he loved and clung to the very things that God warned Israel against – the very things that God asked both leaders and the led to stay far away from were what Solomon held tightly to! Hebrew 1: 9 says:

> *" You have loved righteousness and hated lawlessness; Therefore God, Your God, has anointed You. With the oil of gladness more than Your companions."*

Another subtle way in which seduction works, is to shift or divert a leader from the central focus or main core values of the organization, as well as her real priorities.

The seduced leader may still be talking about the main things, but the allocation of resources - both his own personal resources and that of the organization, especially time and money can easily been seen to have shifted. The focus now is, or where the hearts are tending towards are now different. Again, the story of King Solomon can help us.

Initially, on becoming a king, Solomon's priority was a humble request for wisdom to lead God's people Israel. Solomon also asked God for a heart that will not only distinguish between good and evil, but also choose that which was good and right in God's sight. In response, God gave Solomon beyond what he asked for. As time went on, Solomon had a shift in focus, and he began to allocate resources to new priorities including his numerous wives from foreign lands, as well as their gods! Since every man has a maximum of twenty-four hours in a day, the more Solomon acquired foreign women as wives, and as concubines, the more the time he needed to allocate to them and their pets – the building of 'befitting temples and shrines for their gods. Of course, of necessity; Solomon must follow his wives to worship their gods in their shrines. I perceive one of these women became so audacious and defying that one day she asked Solomon for a space right on Mount Olives so she could erect a temple for her god, and she had her way through. Over time, the skyline of the city of Jerusalem became saturated with pinnacles of shrines erected to several pagan and foreign gods. It is not unlikely too, that one or two buildings previously used to worship the true God were converted to shrines, a situation that must have provoked the hot anger of YAHWEH – the Holy One of Israel!

Today, many a seduced leader don't multiply wives or build shrines for them. Yet, they have gone into, and multiplied projects, buildings, edifices (perhaps educational, social, cities, towers), and other assets which they prioritize.

Can a seduced leader be helped? The answer is YES! God in His infinite mercy will often send His agent to alert and warn such a leader. God may also allow external forces to 'rock the boat' of such a leader, the structures and operations of the organization he or she leads, so as to jolt them into consciousness and wake them up from their slumber. Unfortunately only a few would hear and retrace their steps. This is perhaps where king David was different from many leaders across many generations. In Psalm 51, after the gravity of his sins towards the man Uriah and his wife dawned on him, the man David repented and asked God to create in him a new heart, and also renew the right spirit within him. His son Solomon never did that.

What then are some of the consequences of Seduction? They include disobedience, disloyalty, rejection, and ultimate regret. In some cases, it can lead to loss of position and privileges, and premature death.

# THE BANE
# OF LEADERSHIP II

**Sycophancy and Flattery:**

One of the challenges of leadership in the world today, is the shortage of sincere counsel. To the undoing of many, the allure of office has proved to have a strong corrupting influence on many people around great leaders. Ministers of God are not excluded in this trap. Not too long after introduction to the corridors of power, the best of men and women can begin to experience sycophancy and flattery. Then systematic manipulation soon sets in. As a result, most leaders today are either starved of the truth or presented with filtered, edited or coloured versions of it. The Bible refers to this act as "holding the truth in unrighteousness" (Romans 1:18). Those behind this deception often claim to be acting in the best interest of their masters. They claim that keeping bad news away from the leaders would reduce their exposure to stress.

Thanks be to God for the Holy Spirit who always strengthens and guides His children into all truth! There is therefore no need to filter the truth presented to leaders who are truly operating under God's unction.

Sycophants and flatterers who are in the habit of editing or suppressing the truth are definitely working in the interest of their masters, not God! This practice is a terrible act before God, and Roman 1: 18 tells us that God's wrath is against those who perpetrate it. Armed with the knowledge that any decision based on "truth held back in unrighteousness", would likely be faulty, leaders in all spheres of life have the responsibility of ensuring that they are furnished with the truth at all times. Leaders should therefore endeavour to eliminate the dross of sycophancy. Until then, they may not come forth fully as vessels of honour for the success of their God-given assignment. Whenever a leader works with the raw material of pure truth, with the help of the Holy Spirit, the end product is always a perfect result that is pleasing and acceptable to God.

Talking about 'truth, the Writer of "Empty Truth"[2] said:
"In the Bible, Truth is presented as the nature of God which is

opposed to falsehood, deception and lies. As Paul demonstrates in Romans 9:1, whenever truth is in operation, there is agreement between the human conscience and the witness of the Holy Spirit. Living a life of truth is desirable by God, and receives commendation from Him (Prov 12:22). God is the essence of truth, and He expects this nature of His to reflect in the character of His children. He condemns falsehood in all its forms, but takes pleasure in truth and honesty, which He regards as the hallmark of an upright person.

Truth always paints the picture of things without filtering them to suit personal preferences or vested interests.

**A Little Leaven:**
> *"He who spares his rod hates his son, But he who loves him disciplines him promptly.... Correct your son, and he will give you rest; Yes, he will givede light to your soul. Your glorying is not good. Do you not know that a little leaven leavens the whole lump? Therefore purge out the old leaven, that you may be a new lump, since you truly are unleavened. For indeed Christ, our Passover, was sacrificed for us"*
> **(Proverbs 13:24; 29:17; I Corinthians 5:6-7)**

Anyone - be he a father or leader in secular or religious organization who wants to reach his goal in life must make it a duty to rebuke young and upcoming ones around or under them whenever such younger ones err. The purpose is to cultivate in them, righteous values. Such corrections will also help to shape their destinies. Failure to do so will have several negative consequences - both for the father/leader, and the son and followers. Any attempt by a father/leader to pamper or overlook the evil behaviours of his/her wards, will be a deliberate investment that will bring sorrow in old age (Prov 29:15, 17). The Bible went further that even God did not spare His own Son:

> *"He who did not spare His own Son, but delivered Him up for us all, how shall He not with Him also freely give us all things?"*
>
> **Romans 8:32.**

Very often, as I read the Bible, and I see evil becoming the order of the day, I ask myself some questions: 'How did it begin? Who started it? Who were the agents in spreading it? I believe all the answers to these questions are found in the Bible text earlier quoted:

> *"Do you not know that a little leaven leavens the whole lump? Therefore purge out the old leaven, that you may be a new lump,."*

Today, modern society and some organizations with vision & potentials for great impact are paying the high price of character erosion, in the form of emerging leaders with little or no character! The cycle is simple: Children or staff who get away with evil acts or are allowed to have their way, will succeed in making disciples of their own kind. As time goes on, they will reproduce more quickly, fill up the organization, and even succeed in stiffening the good/diligent and upright ones!

** (There is a much fuller discussion on the subject of 'A Little Leaven' later in this book).

# THE BANE
# OF LEADERSHIP III

**E**verlasting leadership' or self-perpetuation:** This bane makes a leader to see himself or herself as an 'everlasting leader'. Such perception moves the leader to want to self-perpetuate himself or herself. This common feature in African political terrain, is gradually flowing into Christian leadership. Many a political leader in Africa do not think of or plan for succession. Some have been seen to die in office, while some have had to be forced out of office due to ineptitude of old age and ill-health! Some even cleverly work their biological children to take over, while some for the fear of their evil and corrupt practices decide to change the constitutions that brought them to power to their advantage. The truth is that no man or leader is everlasting. Every man or leader has a season and a tenure

(Ecclesiastics 3:1; John 5:33-37; Acts 13:36). Not unrelated to the myth of 'everlasting' leadership, is the bane of a leader being perceived as so unique, and therefore, indispensable. The truth is that while God in his wisdom had over the ages gifted and so endowed some leaders with multiple abilities, yet no leader is indispensable - both with God, and for men.

**Presumption:**
This bane has its root in the attempt of the leader to get a God-given Vision done faster, using human method rather than at God's pace, and in God's own way.

Often, this arises out of over familiarity. Here, the spiritual leader knows God so intimately and thinks he knows Him beyond Himself! The spiritual leader thereby over-trusts men, and commits too many things to their hands, even too early, ever before such men are tested and proven.

In Galatians 4:22-3, 29-30 (NLT), we read:
> *"22 The Scriptures say that Abraham had two sons, one from his slave wife and one from his freeborn wife. 23 The son of the slave wife was born in a human attempt to bring about the fulfilment of God's promise. But the son of the freeborn wife was born as God's own fulfillment of his promise.....29 But you are now being persecuted by those who want you to*

> *keep the law, just as Ishmael, the child born by human effort, persecuted Isaac, the child born by the power of the Spirit.*
> *³⁰ But what do the Scriptures say about that? "Get rid of the slave and her son, for the son of the slave woman will not share the inheritance with the free woman's son."*

Many things are started in the spirit, but as time goes on, the flesh takes over. Unless there is a drastic step taken to recover, the end may be disastrous. In Jeremiah 17:9-10, the Bible says:

> *⁹ "The heart is deceitful above all things, And desperately wicked; Who can know it?¹⁰ I, the LORD, search the heart, I test the mind, Even to give every man according to his ways, According to the fruit of his doings."*

Perhaps one of the greatest challenges that many a Christian movement had faced, and are facing today is that so many things, ranging from position, authority, power, money, and even anointing are in so many wrong hands – in the hand of many men and women who had not been truly converted, or if converted, had not grown up or become 'broken'. With so much entrusted to them, contrary to clearly stated Bible injunctions, they are truly behaving to type -they are trampling on the holy things, and turning around to rend those who gave them such

opportunities:
> "Do not give what is holy to the dogs; nor cast your pearls before swine, lest they trample them under their feet, and turn and tear you in pieces."
>
> **(Matthew 7:6).**

The NLT puts it this way:
> "Don't waste what is holy on people who are unholy. Don't throw your pearls to pigs! They will trample the pearls, then turn and attack you."
>
> **(Matthew 7:6)**

If there is any where this evil trend had been so obvious and pervading, it is in missions fields. If these 'unbroken' vessels by their in-fighting, open rebellion against authorities and superior officers, etc, are just misrepresenting their denominations, it would be of little or no concern. However, the hurts, injuries, and damages that they have caused the Christian body is immeasurable. The situation can be compared with a country that sends out as ambassadors, citizens who are unschooled and ungroomed in international relations and diplomacy. If they are not recalled early enough, the damages they would have done could set the nation back several decades! Part of the way out of this dilemma is to go back to the Scriptures, and reset the rules. This however will not be without some huge costs.

**Obstinacy:**

Another serious bane of leadership is obstinacy or to be obstinate. Obstinacy is to stubbornly adhere to an opinion, a purpose, or course, in spite of reason, arguments or persuasion. To be obstinate is to be adamant and not easily remedied or subdued or removed.

Going through the Scriptures, it becomes clear that there are two sides to the issue - a positive side and a negative side.

In Romans 4:18-20 (NLT), the Bible described Abraham:
> *"[18] Even when there was no reason for hope, Abraham kept hoping—believing that He would become the father of many nations. For God had said to him, "That's how many descendants you will have!"*
> *[19] And Abraham's faith did not weaken, even though, at about 100 years of age, He figured his body was as good as dead—and so was Sarah's womb.*
> *[20] Abraham never wavered in believing God's promise. In fact, his faith grew stronger, and in this He brought glory to God."*

This obvious positive obstinacy paid him off. The Bible told us the basis for this stand of Abraham:
> *"[21] He was fully convinced that God is able to do whatever He promises."*

The same positive obstinacy can also be seen in the life of Paul the Apostle, who in spite of human and even prophetic persuasions, refused and still went to Jerusalem:

> *"$^{10}$ And as we stayed many days, a certain prophet named Agabus came down from Judea. $^{11}$ When he had come to us, he took Paul's belt, bound his own hands and feet, and said, "Thus says the Holy Spirit, 'So shall the Jews at Jerusalem bind the man who owns this belt, and deliver him into the hands of the Gentiles.'"$^{12}$ Now when we heard these things, both we and those from that place pleaded with him not to go up to Jerusalem. $^{13}$ Then Paul answered, "What do you mean by weeping and breaking my heart? For I am ready not only to be bound, but also to die at Jerusalem for the name of the Lord Jesus."$^{14}$ So when he would not be persuaded, we ceased, saying, "The will of the Lord be done."*
>
> (Acts 21:10-14)

Our main focus here is on the negative side of obstinacy – where the leader ignores all physical, tested principles of leadership, and intentionally becomes blind even to the voice of God, and thinks that things will just sort itself out, until the situation almost gets out of hand! A friend reminded me recently, that God gives vision to man, but expects him to work out the details using or receiving counsels from men and women He graciously surrounded him with. At a critical time in His life and ministry, Moses, a great Biblical leader in the Old Testament, had Jethro his father-in-law on hand. Thank God that Moses did not ignore Jethro's advise. It prolonged his life and ministry tenure.

The Apostles in the early history of the church, faced a leadership crisis which was created by the explosion in church growth. They took a resolute decision:

> *"Now in those days, when the number of the disciples was multiplying, there arose a complaint against the Hebrews by the Hellenists, because their widows were neglected in the daily distribution. ² Then the twelve summoned the multitude of the disciples and said, "It is not desirable that we should leave the word of God and serve tables. ³ Therefore, brethren, seek out from among you seven men of good reputation, full of the Holy Spirit and wisdom, whom we may appoint over this business; ⁴ but we will give ourselves continually to prayer and to the ministry of the word."*
>
> **(Acts 6:1-4)**

They Got the burden off their neck, and gave it to seven Deacons. The result was a further explosion in the growth of Disciples, and the Church.

This bane of obstinacy has not only plateaued some organizations – both secular and religious, it has in fact led to their decline and ultimate break up or death of organizations.

**What is the solution here?**
First is to know and truly understand the seemingly simplistic fact that God is God! Also, that God is a highly principled God who is no respecter of persons (Acts 10:34-35).

Second, that it is in the interest of every leader to be conversant with historical antecedents and trends- both biblical and contemporary. In a discussion on the subject of "Wisdom for Better approach", a great Teacher of God's WORD, said "Until a person is willing to review his or her approach, he or she can not improve on results." He went further, "Thank God for where you are, but don't ever stay there, or else you will lose relevance. Therefore, seek for better ways of doing things, and
You will go forward"[3]

# LOST SHEPHERD VS THE LOST SHEEP

*"Then Jesus said to the woman, "I was sent only to help God's lost sheep—the people of Israel."*
**(Matthew 15:24 NLT).**

The background to the above quoted Text are in the two preceding Verses. A woman was in desperate need of deliverance for her daughter who was under severe demonic assault. Jesus 'deliberately ignored' her. The Disciples advised their Master to get rid of her because she was already becoming a nuisance! Then Jesus spoke to the woman: '<u>I was sent only to help God's lost sheep—the people of Israel.</u>" Our focus here is on the phrase: 'GOD's LOST SHEEP - THE PEOPLE OF ISRAEL'.

Hence in this Chapter, we will be addressing the following issues:
- First, that God is a Shepherd.
- Second, there are possibilities that a Sheep can be lost. even more than one sheep can be lost.
- Third, there are possibilities also that someone called to be a Shepherd could be lost!
- Fourth, the circumstances under which a sheep or the Shepherd can be lost. Fifth, the predicament of a lost sheep and a lost Shepherd.
- Finally, we will be asking the twin questions: Am I a lost Sheep who is under and still lovingly obeying and hero-worshipping a lost Shepherd? Or, as a leader, am I a lost Shepherd?

The main call of a Shepherd is to lead and care for the Sheep. A Shepherd is therefore a leader.

In Psalm 23:1, the Psalmist wrote:
*"The Lord is my Shepherd I shall not want."*

Our God is a Shepherd - a good Shepherd, He has several Sheep. As a good Shepherd, God leads, guides, and guards His Sheep. He also nourishes His Sheep. He has several Sheep spread across the whole world. As a good Shepherd He adequately cares for them all. (John 10:14-16)

Though God is a good and loving Shepherd, yet there are possibilities that a Sheep could be lost!

A Sheep could get tired of the abundance of provision under a good Shepherd, and decide to go and see the 'other side' of life. The Prodigal Son was like that. He was 'spoilt' by the overwhelming loving care of his father. Then one day, he decided to bolt away. To prevent any remote control or monitoring, the Bible recorded that he travelled to 'a far country'. He later discovered that life on the other side was hell. Thank God, the Bible said:

> *"But when he had spent all, there arose a severe famine in that land, and he began to be in want.* $^{15}$*Then he went and joined himself to a citizen of that country, and he sent him into his fields to feed swine.* $^{16}$ *And he would gladly have filled his stomach with the pods that the swine ate, and no one gave him anything.* $^{17}$ *"<u>But when he came to himself</u>, he said, 'How many of my father's hired servants have bread enough and to spare, and I perish with hunger!* $^{18}$*I will arise and go to my father, and will say to him, "Father, I have sinned against heaven and before you,* $^{19}$ *and I am no longer worthy to be called your son. Make me like one of your hired servants."'*

> [20] *"And he arose and came to his father. But when he was still a great way off, his father saw him and had compassion, and ran and fell on his neck and kissed him.* [21] *And the son said to him, 'Father, I have sinned against heaven and in your sight, and am no longer worthy to be called your son.'"*
>
> **(Luke 15:16-21).**

A Sheep could also get lost through evil association. I once heard the story of two married women. They had been friends from their days in the Secondary School. Once married, they got used to comparing notes especially on how well each of their husbands was taking care of his wife. We will call them "Mrs A" and "Mrs B". Mrs A married a very top Civil Servant, while Mrs B was married to a top Military officer. Mr A did pretty well in always releasing a reasonable amount of money to his wife for upkeep. On the other hand, the soldier in Mr B would not let him care as much for his family, even though he was better paid and far richer than Mr A. Mrs B got jealous of her friend, and started framing up stories that her husband (Mr B) was always giving her far more than Mrs A was getting from her husband. Over time, Mrs A started pestering the life of her husband, taunting him until the man got fed up and asked her to pack out! Not long after, Mrs B started befriending Mr A, which Mrs A got to know about. However, it was already too late for Mrs A to recover her husband. At the end, the friendship of Mrs A and Mrs B got broken. In fact, they fought somewhere in the public to the extent of tearing each other's dresses! I Corinthians 15:33 says:

*"Evil communications corrupt good manners."*

The GNB puts it this way:
*"Don't be deceived, evil friends will destroy you"!*

As that truth applies to a sheep, so it does to a Shepherd too. In wanting to grow their Ministry or church – both in attendance and in finances with a resultant hope to boost their fame and ego, many a Shepherd have veered off the truth they once stood upon. They have joined association and groups whose doctrines and ways of doing Ministry are questionable. Some have acquired titles, become occultic, and resorted to magic. It is said that many who go around in flowing gowns, wearing shining rings on their fingers, or wave their so-called 'anointed handkerchiefs, are already lost shepherds who had been busy dining and wining with the devil (see I Kings 18:19). In some extreme cases, some have sacrificed their spouses or firstborn child to get the so called 'power of God!

Now, let's take a look at the predicament of a lost Sheep, as well as a lost Shepherd.

The story of the Prodigal Son (referred to above), vividly described the predicament of a lost Sheep. The only way out is for them to come to their senses and return home to God in genuine repentance.

For the lost Shepherd, I believe the story of Samson (in Judges 16: 16-22), has some lessons. Know where you derailed, forget your reputation, fame and popularity. Get a quiet and solitary place, fall upon your face and cry out to God for mercy and forgiveness – both for yourself, and for the multitude you may have deceived and misled.

Remember, when the 'moment of truth' comes, and you stand alone before your Maker to give account of your life, it will be you and you alone. Which verdict would you want to hear on that day? – "Welcome, thou good and faithful servant", or "Depart from Me, ye workers of iniquity".

> *"He also who had received two talents came and said,'Lord, you delivered to me two talents; look, I have gained two more talents besides them.' His lord said to him, 'Well done, good and faithful servant; you have been faithful over a few things, I will make you ruler over many things. Enter into the joy of your lord.'". "Not everyone who says to Me, 'Lord, Lord,' shall enter the kingdom of heaven, but he who does the will of My Father in heaven. Many will say to*

*Me in that day, 'Lord, Lord, have we not prophesied in Your name, cast out demons in Your name, and done many wonders in Your name?'* [23] *And then I will declare to them, 'I never knew you; depart from Me, you who practice lawlessness!'"*

**(Matthew 25:22-23; Matthew 7:21-23).**

# A LITTLE LEAVEN

*"Your glorying is not good. Do you not know that a little leaven leavens the whole lump? Therefore purge out the old leaven, that you may be a new lump, since you truly are unleavened. For indeed Christ, our Passover, was sacrificed for us. Therefore let us keep the feast, not with old leaven, nor with the leaven of malice and wickedness, but with the unleavened bread of sincerity and truth"....... "A little leaven leavens the whole lump. I have confidence in you, in the Lord, that you will have no other mind; but he who troubles you shall bear his judgment, whoever he is."*

**(I Corinthians 5:6-9; Galatians 5:9).**

A leaven has been described as a substance or material that is used to produce fermentation or gas that lightens or modifies, a dough. It also has the capacity to mingle with or permeate the totality of anything it comes in contact with. In other words, a leaven has the power to positively add value to, or to negatively devalue anything it touches. It's power to affect positively or negatively is not in its size but in its influence. If positive, a leaven can, like salt and light be a blessing. On the other hand, if negative, a leaven, like poison, could bring down a great and powerful organization. Also to be noted is that the bigger the 'dough' to which the leaven is out to permeate, the greater the blessing, or damage, depending on whether the leaven is positive or negative. For the purpose of our discussion in this Chapter, perhaps one can add that not only are there old and new leaven, there are also good and evil leavens!

In Genesis 1:26-28, the first Godhead-in-Council Meeting was called. It was a positive leaven being introduced into the Creation:

> *"Then God said, "Let Us make man in Our image, according to Our likeness; let them have dominion over the fish of the sea, over the birds of the air, and over the cattle, over all the earth and over every creeping thing that creeps on the earth." So God created man in His own image; in the image of God*

*He created him; male and female He created them. Then God blessed them, and God said to them, "Be fruitful and multiply; fill the earth and subdue it; have dominion over the fish of the sea, over the birds of the air, and over every living thing that moves on the earth.""*

In Genesis 11:1-9, we hear of another leaven being introduced. This time, it was a negative leaven:

*"Now the whole earth had one language and one speech. And it came to pass, as they journeyed from the east, that they found a plain in the land of Shinar, and they dwelt there. Then they said to one another, "Come, let us make bricks and bake them thoroughly." They had brick for stone, and they had asphalt for mortar. And they said, "Come, let us build ourselves a city, and a tower whose top is in the heavens; let us make a name for ourselves, lest we be scattered abroad over the face of the whole earth." But the Lord came down to see the city and the tower which the sons of men had built. And the Lord said, "Indeed the people are one and they all have one language, and this is what they begin to do; now nothing that they propose to do will be withheld from them. Come, let Us go down and there confuse their language, that they may not understand one*

*another's speech." So the Lord scattered them abroad from there over the face of all the earth, and they ceased building the city. Therefore its name is called Babel, because there the Lord confused the language of all the earth; and from there the Lord scattered them abroad over the face of all the earth."*

Our Lord Jesus, in Matthew 5:13-16, said His Disciples (all true and genuine Christians), are the salt of the earth, as well as the Light of the world. In several places in the Bible, Christians are warned against wrong associations and evil influences (Psalm 1:1-3; Proverbs 1:10-19; I Corinthians 15:33, etc).

Apostle Paul, also in his Epistles to the Churches in Corinth and Galatia, pointed out that there are two types of leaven - an old and a new. He alerted on the danger which a negative leaven poses to a whole loaf or body (especially a group of Christians). He then went on to admonish Christians to purge themselves.

In Revelation 2: 12-15, the Lord Jesus accused the Church in Pergamum, of the leaven they accepted, tolerated, and allowed to permeate them. This caused untold damage to the church – both as individuals, as families, as a denomination, and a Body of Christ in that City! What is this telling us? Simple, any little compromise or evil we accept or allow, will like cancer, eventually spread, permeate and become big, with the ultimate power to kill and destroy the entire body or church system.

What are you tolerating? In Luke 16:15, Jesus told the Pharisees:
*"And He said to them, "You are those who justify yourselves before men, but God knows your hearts. For what is highly esteemed among men is an abomination in the sight of God."*

Do you impose your will and desire on and above the word of God? Do you justify yourself in evil? The earlier you repent, the better for you. Are you a leader of some sort, and you are pampering evil doers? Watch, if you don't take firm, serious and urgent actions against such perpetrators, it is a matter of time, they will destroy all you have laboured to build!

The statement of our Lord in Revelation 2:15 is particularly very instructive: "In *a similar way, you have some Nicolaitans among you who follow the same teaching."* **(NLT)**

'You have some Nicholaitans among you who follow'. Every 'some' – whether for good or for evil, always start or begin with one person. Every evil that has become major issues or destructive activities in today's church, began with or was introduced by one person. Because colleagues, superiors and leaders – both immediate and at the top allowed, tolerated, or closed their eyes to these evil, and with time, they became the order of the day! This is why it is critical for everyone to be his Brother's keeper, otherwise everyone will eventually be caught up in the web. Unfortunately, the damage would already have been done.

Again, Apostle Paul, in II Timothy 2: 19-26, wrote:
*"Nevertheless the solid foundation of God stands, having this seal: "The Lord knows those who are His," and, "Let everyone who names the name of Christ depart from iniquity."But in a great house there are not only vessels of gold and silver, but also of wood and clay, some for honour and some for dishonour. Therefore if anyone cleanses himself from the latter, he will be a vessel for honour, sanctified and useful for the Master, prepared for every good work. Flee also youthful lusts; but pursue righteousness, faith, love, peace with those who call on the Lord out of a pure heart. But avoid foolish and ignorant disputes, knowing that they generate strife. And a servant of the Lord must not quarrel but be gentle to all, able to teach, patient, in humility correcting those who are in opposition, if God perhaps will grant them repentance, so that they may know the truth, and that they may come to their senses and escape the snare of the devil, having been taken captive by him to do his will."*

# LEADERSHIP & SUCCESSION

# LEADERSHIP & SUCCESSION

| | |
|---|---|
| 2.1 | Succession- God's Own Idea |
| 2.2 | Leadership & Succession |
| 2.3 | Leadership Transition |
| 2.4 | Joshua – A Leadership Post-Mortem |
| 2.5 | Where Are The Jethro Fathers? |

# SUCCESSION - GOD'S OWN IDEA

*"In the beginning God created the heavens and the earth. " Then God said, "Let the earth bring forth grass, the herb that yields seed, and the fruit tree that yields fruit according to its kind, whose seed is in itself, on the earth"; and it was so. " And the earth brought forth grass, the herb that yields seed according to its kind, and the tree that yields fruit, whose seed is in itself according to its kind. And God saw that it was good."*

**Succession has been variously described as:**
The order or sequence of inheriting of a title, office, power (especially of a royal title)'.

- The order in which, or the conditions under which one person after another succeeds to a property, dignity, title or throne.
- A group of people or things arranged or following in order.'
- The act or process of one person taking the place of another in the enjoyment or liability for right or duties, or both.

In most cases, the primary purpose of succession is to facilitate the continuance of the corporate personality.

Inherent, and perhaps also clearly revealed in the Creation story of the Book of Genesis 1, and in all that God made, and especially the blessing He pronounced on man, was the issue of Succession. Hence, everything God made – from vegetation (plants and trees), to sea creatures (both great and small), to animals, and more importantly, man had a divinely-arranged order of replacing or succeeding itself.

Since institutions and organizations – both human and spiritual, are meant to exist for some considerable length of time- often outliving their initiators, and founding fathers, it becomes necessary as long as they thrive, to be intentional in ensuring smooth transition from one leadership regime to another.

This transition should be well planned, and protected from any possible manipulation by a leader or his/her sycophants who may want to perpetuate them.

# LEADERSHIP & SUCCESSION

*"After the death of Moses the servant of the LORD, it came to pass that the LORD spoke to Joshua the son of Nun, Moses' assistant, saying: <sup>2</sup> "Moses My servant is dead. Now therefore, arise, go over this Jordan, you and all this people, to the land which I am giving to them—the children of Israel. <sup>3</sup> Every place that the sole of your foot will tread upon I have given you, as I said to Moses. From the wilderness and thisLebanon as far as the great river, the River Euphrates, all the land of the Hittites, and to the Great Sea toward the going down of the sun, shall be your territory. <sup>5</sup> No man shall be able to stand before you all the days of your life; as I was with Moses, so I*

*will be with you. I will not leave you nor forsake you."*

**(Joshua 1:1-5)**

An adage says "It is the egg that precedes the hen, even as the caterpillar precedes the butterfly " Perhaps it may also be the other way round, as without the hen or the butterfly, there may never have been an egg or the caterpillar in the first place!

Most of the challenges and problems which Christianity and the Church are facing globally today, can be traced back to one primary source – lack of Biblical and true discipleship in today's Churches. There is a wide gap between what the Church was in the New Testament, and what we have today. Until we understand and correct the missing link, the Church – its members and the leaders they ultimately become, will remain a group of shallow, timid, and defeated soldiers in the army of Jesus.

**Ezekiel 33:12-15 says:**

*[12] "Therefore you, O son of man, say to the children of your people: 'The righteousness of the righteous man shall not deliver him in the day of his transgression; as for the wickedness of the wicked, he shall not fall because of it in the day that he turns from his*

*wickedness; nor shall the righteous be able to live because of his righteousness in the day that he sins.' [13] When I say to the righteous that he shall surely live, but he trusts in his own righteousness and commits iniquity, none of his righteous works shall be remembered; but because of the iniquity that he has committed, he shall die. [14] Again, when I say to the wicked, 'You shall surely die,' if he turns from his sin and does what is lawful and right, [15] if the wicked restores the pledge, gives back what he has stolen, and walks in the statutes of life without committing iniquity, he shall surely live; he shall not die."*

From this passage, it becomes clear that the raw material for church members and the church leaders are the sinners. In witnessing to, and getting the sinners converted, they (the Sinners) must be told to:
- Turn from their sins,
- Begin to do what is lawful and right in the sight of God – according to His written word – the Holy Bible,
- Restore the pledge (i.e honour their words and vows),
- Give back again to the owner, what he had robbed him of (i.e, restitute their past),
- Walk in the statutes of life (not of death),
- No more commit iniquity.

In summary, to become a new creature in Christ, the sinner must genuinely repent and begin to bear the fruit of repentance (Luke 3:7-9, NLT):

> *"7 When the crowds came to John for baptism, He said, "You brood of snakes! Who warned you to flee God's coming wrath? 8 Prove by the way you live that you have repented of your sins and turned to God. Don't just say to each other, 'We're safe, for we are descendants of Abraham.' That means nothing, for I tell you, God can create children of Abraham from these very stones. 9 Even now the axe of God's judgment is poised, ready to sever the roots of the trees. Yes, every tree that does not produce good fruit will be chopped down and thrown into the fire."*

All the above listed actions and way of living will only be possible if we (the genuine and committed Christians, as well as leaders), get people converted and we do all we can to also disciple them. If there is no genuine conversion, there will be no genuine discipleship. Consequently, there will be no genuine and true biblical leaders in the Church!

What was the pattern of discipleship adopted by the Lord Jesus, and which His own Disciples followed, and which He asked to be taught and done in all places even unto the end of age?

Let's look at Mark 3:13-15:

> *"¹³ And He went up on the mountain and called to Him those He Himself wanted. And they came to Him. ¹⁴ Then He appointed twelve, that they might be with Him and that He might send them out to preach, ¹⁵ and to have power to heal sicknesses and to cast out demons:"*

In this passage, the Lord Jesus called the people who were later named Disciples, first to be with Him so they could learn of Him. Thereafter, He empowered and sent them out to do what they had seen Him do. It is worthy of note that when these Disciples returned, they testified of the great things God did with and through them. In return, Jesus gave them more powers, and of course, He warned them to focus on the ultimate and most important reason for their salvation which is making it to Heaven and also reigning with our Lord Jesus Christ.

Luke 10:17-19, 20-21 tell us:

> *"¹⁷ Then the seventy returned with joy, saying, "Lord, even the demons were subject to us in Your name."¹⁸ And He said to them, "I saw Satan fall like lightning from heaven. ¹⁹ Behold, I give you the authority to trample on serpents and scorpions, and over all the power of the enemy, and nothing shall by any means*

*hurt you. ²⁰Nevertheless do not rejoice in this, that the spirits are subject to you, but rather rejoice because your names are written in heaven."…..²¹ In that hour Jesus rejoiced in the Spirit and said, "I thank You, Father, Lord of heaven and earth, that You have hidden these things from the wise and prudent and revealed them to babes. Even so, Father, for so it seemed good in Your sight."*

Also, in Mark 16:15-17, we read:

*"¹⁵ And He said to them, "Go into all the world and preach the gospel to every creature. ¹⁶ He who believes and is baptized will be saved; but he who does not believe will be condemned.*

*¹⁷ And these signs will follow those who believe: In My name they will cast out demons; they will speak with new tongues;"*

Here, Our Lord Jesus asked us to preach, teach (what He had commanded us), and to make disciples of all Nations.

The core of the problems lies in the fact that in many places, we teach or instruct people on <u>what</u> to do, BUT we don't show them <u>how</u> to. So, at best many Christians carry a lot of Bible knowledge in their heads, but little in their hearts. Many, perhaps can be said to be suffering from spiritual constipation! Since they lack the 'how' to do 'what' they know, they cannot raise people to do same.

One of the ways out is to adopt and begin to use the three concepts of "SHAPE, "SOAP" and "LIFE".[4]

The 'SHAPE' helps us to discover our fit in the body of Christ. The 'SOAP' helps us to read, observe, and prayerfully apply the Scriptures to our daily life. The LIFE journaling helps us maintain a regular and systematic daily life with the word of God.(See more on LIFE, SOAP & SHAPE under "Appendices", at the end of this Book).

It is good to emphasize or reiterate that 'Succession' and 'Succession planning' are godly concepts. They are Biblical, and they enhance God's plan and agenda. They are not carnal, or restricted to secular leaders or leadership. It should therefore be pursued by every godly leader and every godly organization.

Succession is inherent in the mandate which God gave to man in Gen 1:26-28. In fact it is a very vital tool to get that Divine mandate fulfilled!

**Succession and the Creation Mandate:**
Right from the very Beginning -at Creation, God blessed the

man He created in His own image and likeness. That singular blessing is unique in many respects. The Bible says:

> *"26 And God said, Let us make man in our image, after our likeness: and let them have dominion over the fish of the sea, and over the fowl of the air, and over the cattle, and over all the earth, and over every creeping thing that creepeth upon the earth. 27 So God created man in his own image, in the image of God created he him; male and female created he them. 28 And God blessed them, and God said unto them, Be fruitful, and multiply, and replenish the earth, and subdue it: and have dominion over the fish of the sea, and over the fowl of the air, and over every living thing that moveth upon the earth."*
>
> **(Genesis 1:26-28)**

- it is the first blessing that God ever pronounced. Before He did that, He, the Almighty God, had only been saying 'and it was good'.

- this peculiar Blessing had four dimensions - we are to be (i.e, be and become) fruitful, multiply, replenish the earth and subdue it".

Before looking into the details of each of these Divine blessings, it is worthy of note that ALL fruitfulness, increases and multiplications - whether in plants and animals had been due to this initial blessing that God pronounced at Creation.

It is that same Blessing which had allowed the human race to be perpetuated. As (and before) one generation passes away, another one appears. In fact, the outgoing generation always gives birth to more children, more ideas, more discoveries, and more and newer innovations, that supersede those of the preceding generations)!!! Thank God for the power of His Word (See Genesis 1:28; Psalm 33:8-12; Psalm 119:89; Isaiah 40:8; John 6:63; Hebrews 4:12, etc).

To be fruitful therefore means yielding or producing fruit; to be conducive to an abundant yield; to be abundantly productive. To be fruitful means being productive in every sense, and yielding benefits.

On the other hand, to multiply means to become many, much, more than two, and many times over.

**Biblical Succession:**
God is a God of order. He is also a God of pattern. There is an order, as well as patterns observable in the way He has moved across generations. For example, He has a definite time, place and tenure for every leader He chooses. One day, a

seemingly/apparently unique and great "Moses the Servant of God" will finish his own term and tenure, and die! He must, of necessity leave the scene. BUT the work of God as well as His Kingdom Agenda MUST continue. If it did not end or stop with Abraham, Jacob, Joseph, Moses, Samuel, David, Elijah, Elijah, etc, or EVEN with the Lord Jesus, the Disciples (especially Paul), it WILL NOT stop now - with the departure of any great/unique leader in our own generation. It is the duty and responsibility of a current leader to PUT ALL THINGS (spiritual and human) IN PLACE TO ENSURE that God's Kingdom Agenda continues (Note God's pattern again: God clearly revealed Joshua to Moses; Elisha to Elijah; Timothy and Titus to Paul; etc. He has not changed! Even today, He can clearly reveal a successor to current leaders as need arises)

# LEADERSHIP TRANSITION

*"14 And the LORD said unto Moses, Behold, thy days approach that thou must die: call Joshua, and present yourselves in the tabernacle of the congregation, that I may give him a charge. And Moses and Joshua went, and presented themselves in the tabernacle of the congregation. 15 And the LORD appeared in the tabernacle in a pillar of a cloud: and the pillar of the cloud stood over the door of the tabernacle."*

(Deuteronomy 31: 14-15)

The Heart of the Leader: It is to be noted that before he or she became a leader, the man or woman we now call a leader was, and still is, a man or a woman! Till he or she will leave office, and finally this world, he or she will continue to be a man or a woman. In Jeremiah 17:9, we read:

*"The heart is deceitful above all things, And desperately wicked; Who can know it?"*

It is however expected that over time, and before becoming a leader or reaching the leadership cadre, such a man or woman should have undergone 'heart surgery' and received a brand new heart - the heart of Jesus (Philipians 2:5-11); and the heart of the Father - a heart that wants to see God's Kingdom come, and His will done on the earth as it is in Heaven (Matthew 6:10). There is therefore a strong connection between the head and the heart of the leader. When the two are in different directions, there will be conflict and confusion.

In this chapter, we will be looking at a few conceptual issues. The first is the "Smart Guy" Theory of leadership.

**"Smart Guy" Theory:**
'Smart' Guys, by nature are people who show a high degree of mental ability. They are clever and intelligent. They are needed in every organization. Every leader who wants to succeed need such people. However, if not carefully watched, Smart Guys can

pose serious dangers! One of the ways they operate is that they study the nature of various people in top leadership positions in organizations, especially the organization they operate in. They especially study the weaknesses of such top leaders, and capitalize on them. They either fuel or exploit such weaknesses. For example, if they observed that a leader loves praise, and gifts, they will fully and regularly stuff him or her with all these, even when it is unnecessary or uncalled for. As its often said that 'he who pays the piper dictates the tune', as time goes on, the 'smart guy' begins to call the shots! Even when the leader they already succeeded in 'catching' does not want to see or give 'Smart Guys' attention, they demand it and force their way in. I once overheard a 'Smart Guy' saying, "even the Bible also says 'that the gift of a man makes way for him'"! In other words, 'Smart guys' can easily worm their ways to the hearts of unsuspecting leaders. Hence, 'Smart Guys' can begin to have their ways from unit or Departmental levels, to Divisions, and eventually with the head of their organizations. Worse still is the fact that with time, 'Smart Guys' will start to raise disciples of their own types.

Without any doubt, it can be said that there is a spirit behind such a phenomenon. Perhaps such spirits can be called the "Absalom spirit" (II Samuel 15:1-12). More often than not, 'Smart Guys' present a form of godliness (fake godliness) and uses it as a way to gain (I Timothy 6:6-12, NLT). In the process, they can blackmail, assassinate, and/or eliminate anyone who would not let them have their way. With all the foregoing as his tools, 'Smart Guys' rise fast to the top. The reality however, is that they also fall and crash fast! The reason is simple - as their so called 'gifts' make way for them, the same 'gifts' lead them to the abysses. Their character deficiencies soon come to the surface. While gifts make ways for them, character deficiencies and moral bankruptcy lead them to their Waterloo.

**Vision Vs Ambition:**
The word 'Vision' has different contexts and usages. Among others, it is said to be:
- the act or power of sight; a mental picture of a desired future; some things that are seen in a dream/trance. (Many times the phrase: "in a Vision of the night", is used in the Bible. This could mean what God shows in a dream, or God waking up someone in the night, & HE began to show him or her things).

A Vision is also 'a concern or preparation for the future - foresight); a thought/concept/object formed by the imagination.

Perhaps it will not be out of place here to state that there is a very thin line between 'vision' and 'ambition'. While vision is what God wants a man to be, on the other hand, ambition is what a man chooses to be - with or without God!

Ambition can become a vision, while vision too can become an ambition. A man can bolt away from God's vision. He can also hijack a Godly vision and turn it to his own, thereby using God to fulfil his/her ambition.

One may ask 'How can a vision become ambition?' This can happen when the vision must be achieved at all cost – even if through using some ungodly means or going ahead of God's time-table! For example, God gave King Solomon many big ideas and projects. As time went on, he resorted to taxing the Israelites. When his son, Rehoboam succeeded him, there was a revolt demanding that he (Rehoboth) should scale down the tax. A delegate was sent to him. The Elders gave him a wise counsel to reduce the hardship of the people. He ignored this, but rather chose to follow the advice of his peers – the young men. The result was catastrophic! Rehoboth was outdated as king, and the Nation of Israel broke into two kingdoms. (See I Kings 12:1-24). Man can often use vision to achieve ambition.

Something seem to be interesting about God when it comes to the issue of leadership and succession. As long as man's 'smartness' is working for His glory and it advances His Kingdom agenda, God may not react to the activities and intrigues of the 'Smart' leader. However, when the 'Smart' leader gets to the peak, and God sends him warnings which he refuses to heed, then He, the Almighty and Sovereign One will back out!

Solomon, again fitly illustrates this.

The Question on many lips over the years has been: Where is God, or why does God not caution or prevent a leader when it becomes so obvious that his or her ambition is replacing (or has replaced) Vision? Some even ask: Why in His sovereignty does this Almighty God still make His power to flow with miracles, signs, or even some unprecedented successes still following the one who is now pursuing a personal agenda rather than God's divine will?

I found part of the answers in Psalm 115:3:
> *"But our God is in heaven; He does whatever He pleases."*

God is sovereign- He does as He pleases! He has the prerogative to speak to or be quiet with whoever He chooses - JUST AS IT PLEASES HIM!

Moreover, I also observed that, according to Romans 8:28:
> *"And we know that all things work together for good to those who love God, to those who are the called according to His purpose."*

Before anything can work for the good of any man, it must first have worked for the good of God Himself. The implication of this is that even if a leader (whether a man or woman) has replaced vision with ambition, or has 'cleverly' repackaged and presented or promoted ambition as vision, in as much as it is advancing God's divine purpose, God will show up or back it up for His Namesake! (See Philipians 1:12-26; ...).

The foregoing notwithstanding, God will still keep on sending warning signals to the ambitious leader. The problem however, is that because the heart has already derailed, he/she cannot and will not hear! Someone said everything is a matter of the heart - the <u>shape</u> and st<u>ate</u> of the heart. The heart can open or blind the eyes, the ears, or even the mouth. The shape and state of the heart can give strength to the hand and feet. It can equally weaken both (See Judges 6: 13-15; I Samuel 17:32-37).

In his book, "Merchants In the Temple" (page 68), Gianluigi Nuzzi wrote on the incredible case of Monsignor Nuncio Scaramo. It was a revelation of the kind of men in today's church leadership, and how the mind of the Pope was already made up. In this case, the policy of a soft and decisive revolution prevailed - a tangible sign of the Pope's break with the past![5]

## "The Lost Sheep" Theory of Leadership:
Here, the leader had hitherto been doing well, but suddenly, he or she begins to do some things that can work against the long term interest of the organization.

The leader himself or herself has ceased to be in charge. This could be due to loss of vision that led to loss of focus, or simply due to what one can call' vision hijack'. King Saul is a classical example here. When he failed in his assignment to go and wipe out the Amalekites, his excuse was 'the people'. As a student of strategic leadership, I am an advocate of 'next generation' involvement. However, I often have warned against 'zeal without knowledge.

Hosea 4:6, reads:
> *"My people are destroyed for lack of knowledge. Because you have rejected knowledge, I also will reject you from being priest for Me; Because you have forgotten the law of your God, I also will forget your children." (KJV)*

NLT puts it this way:
> *"My people are being destroyed because they don't know me. Since you priests refuse to know me, I refuse to recognize you as my priests. Since you have forgotten the laws of your God, I will forget to bless your children."*

Here, the Bible shows us clearly three categories of people, as well as the consequences of their actions.

- those who lack knowledge (i.e those who are ignorant), those who reject knowledge (i.e those who refuse and resist the knowledge), and,
- those who forgot the law (they used to know, but now have forgotten what they used to know).

A look around organizations - both secular and religious - shows clearly that we are in the era of 'Smart Guy' leadership, and probably also in an era of lost shepherd, too.

# JOSHUA
*(A Leadership Post-Mortem)*

*"Every place that the sole of your foot will tread uponI have given you, as I said to Moses. From thewilderness and this Lebanon as far as the great river, the River Euphrates, all the land of the Hittites, and to the Great Sea toward the going down of the sun, shall be your territory.". "And it came to pass a long time after that the LORD had given rest unto Israel from all their enemies round about, that Joshua waxed old and stricken in age. 2 And Joshua called for all Israel, and for their elders, and for their heads, and for their judges, and for their officers, and said unto them, I am old and stricken in age:"*

**(Joshua 1:3-4, 23:1-2).**

Here, God spelt out in clear terms what Joshua, the successor to Moses (that great man of God) was called to do. God went to the extent of giving him even the geographical boundaries of the land to be possessed. More importantly however, there were four particular promises of God to Joshua:

(a)   Every place that the soul of your foot will tread upon, I have given you(Vs 3),
(b)   No man shall be able to stand before you all the days of your life (Vs5),
(c)   As I was with Moses, so I will be with you (Vs 5),
(d)   I will not leave you nor forsake you (Vs 5),

Years rolled by, several efforts and conquests were made. Then God showed up again and said something very strange in chapter 13:1 - "Thou art old and well stricken in years, and there remaineth yet very much land to be possessed" (not just to be entered but to be possessed!).

There seem to be a lot of Questions or 'Matters Arising' from this last divine encounter between Joshua and God:
First, what could have happened over the years that even in the old age of Joshua, 'there(still) remained yet very much land to be possessed?"

Second, did God underestimate the assignment, and/or the capability of Joshua, or both?

Third, was there so much diversion, distraction, and dissipation of energy by Joshua on wrong things? For example, settling of quarrels and disputes, etc, to the extent that he, Joshua had little time left for the essentials? In other words, did the urgent prevent Joshua from the important? Perhaps apostle Peter and some Leaders in the early church of the New Testament learnt some lessons from Joshua's case, and this made them to resolutely declare in Acts 6:2-4:

> "*2 Then the twelve called the multitude of the disciples unto them, and said, It is not reason that we should leave the word of God, and serve tables. 3 Wherefore, brethren, look ye out among you seven men of honest report, full of the Holy Ghost and wisdom, whom we may appoint over this business. 4 But we will give ourselves continually to prayer, and to the ministry of the word."*

Fourth, were there so many 'dead woods' in Joshua's team which he refused to get rid of – some people one could refer to as "Executive liabilities"?

Fifth, did little successes limit Joshua from bigger achievements?

Any of the above issues can easily befall a leader, and if not prayerfully and thoughtfully addressed, can prevent a leader from fulfilling God's purpose.

Sixth, did Joshua have some personal challenges that became hindrances to fulfilling destiny? For instance, health, marital, or other related issues.

Are you a leader of some sort? Are you a leader in the home, a leader over a small or large organization? Are you concerned that you are growing old, and succession has become a major issue?

As you weigh your life, and your leadership style or your performance by some of the questions above, may the Holy Spirit enlighten and give you strategies that will help you finish strong, and finish well - without scars, in Jesus Name!

# WHERE ARE THE JETHRO FATHERS'?

*"₁₇ So Moses' father-in-law said to him, "The thing that you do is not good. ₁₈ Both you and these people who are with you will surely wear yourselves out. For this thing is too much for you; you are not able to perform it by yourself. ₁₉ Listen now to my voice; I will give you counsel, and God will be with you: Stand before God for the people, so that you may bring the difficulties to God. ₂₀ And you shall teach them the statutes and the laws, and show them the way in which they must walk and the work they must do."*

**(Exodus 18:17-20)**

Ordinarily it may sound strange and surprising that until the man JETHRO showed up on the scene, God was quiet while Moses slaved away thinking he was an all-in-all to the people. It however points to the fact that God is a principled God.

There are some things that He has put within the purview of man, especially the leaders. If such leaders ignore God's principles, God may rarely intervene. In the case of Moses, the only, if not the last way God could assist him was to send his father-in-law to him.

It behoves every good leader to realize that God has given him or her worthwhile people, and if he or she (the leader) has taken time to lead them well (by his or her life and leadership example), then they should have 'caught his/her spirit' (Philipians 4:9).

Also, it is in the interest of the leader to delegate assignments and responsibilities to tested and proven hands. In addition, the leader should begin delegating very early, after training the people. This adequately follows the example of our Lord Jesus who sent out the Twelve on many occasions before He finally sent them out as He went to Heaven. Apostle Paul too did the same.(See Mark 3:13-15; Matt 10:1-26; Luke 10:1-19; Luke 24:49;

John 20:21; Acts 1:8). It is wisdom for a leader to have regular retreats with those to whom he delegated assignments so as to have the opportunity to evaluate performance, correct errors, recast vision, and refire them. Finally, the leader needs to realize that leading or leadership is for a season (Ecclesiastics 3:1). No leader can be there forever. The truth is, if a leader wants to hold on, or does not want to leave, when his or her season is over, men, being who they are, would naturally leave to seek a new leader:

> *"³³In fact, you sent investigators to listen to John the Baptist, and his testimony about me was true. ³⁴ Of course, I have no need of human witnesses, but I say these things so you might be saved. ³⁵ John was like a burning and shining lamp, and you were excited for a while about his message."*
> **(John 5:33-35, NLT)**

In prescribing what should be done, father Jethro gave some practical Action Steps to Moses the great man of God,(and in effect, to every wise leader):

+ stand before God for the people - so you may bring their difficulties to God(- the problems, issues, challenges, etc that are beyond them, and even beyond you their leader).

+ teach them (the people, and especially your lieutenants), the statutes and the laws of the Lord.

- + show them the way in which they must walk, and the work they must do (i.e, give them a manual of operations, and not just Guidelines)!⁶

- + select from all the people (know who to delegate to):
  - able men
  - such as fear God (i.e people who have character and are also competent, not charisma + competence!)
  - men of truth (those who are honest, have integrity, etc).
  - men who hate covetousness. (they are there to serve, and not for gain)!

- + place them within their known capacity (don't give them beyond what they can cope with or else they become overwhelmed, intoxicated (power and/or money drunk, proud and arrogant)... Recall the Parable of the Talents - 5,2,1.

- + Appoint rulers of 1000s; rulers of 100s; rulers of 50s; and rulers of 10s.

Thank God that Moses heeded the counsel of his father-in-law, resulting in a more fruitful and longer life!

# BUILDING TO LAST

# BUILDING TO LAST

| 3.1 | Building To Last |
| 3.2 | The Successful Leader |
| 3.3 | The Sons of Eli |
| 3.4 | "In the Days of Samuel" |
| 3.5 | Catching the Spirit of the Leader (Finishing Well) |

# BUILDING TO LAST

*"I value self-discipline, but creating systems that make it next to impossible to misbehave is more reliable than self control"* - **Tim Ferriss**[7]
*"Unless the Lord builds the house, They labor in vain who build it; Unless the Lord guards the city, The watchman stays awake in vain."*
(Psalm 127:1)

To build is to construct. Construction is preceded by having a plan, getting the right materials, and an expert to handle the project. Then comes the issues of foundation, structure, etc.

In life, we endeavor to build several things – both physical and spiritual. We attempt to build careers, homes, future and destinies. We also try to build Ministries, Nations, etc.

God is a Builder - a Master Architect and a Master Builder.
If what we are trying to build will last, then we must pay attention to some things.

For example, the ground upon which we are building, the foundation we are laying for what we are trying to build, the materials we are using in building what is being built, and so on and so forth (Psalm 127:1; II Thessalonians 3:6-12; Matthew 7:24-27; I Corinthians 3:-12).

In organizations, when we talk about building to last, it is critical to look far into the future. This is because the weaknesses of leaders, and what they are trying to build rarely show up until much later in their lifetime, or in the life of the organization. In some cases, not until about 5-10 years after many of the leaders may have gone (I Kings 12:1-24)!

In Genesis 35: 1-5, we read:
> *Then God said to Jacob, "Get ready and move to Bethel and settle there. Build an altar there to the God who appeared to you when you fled from your brother, Esau."*

*[2]So Jacob told everyone in his household, "Get rid of all your pagan idols, purify yourselves, and put on clean clothing.[3]We are now going to Bethel, where I will build an altar to the God who answered my prayers when I was in distress. He has been with me wherever I have gone."[4]So they gave Jacob all their pagan idols and earrings, and he buried them under the great tree near Shechem. [5]As they set out, a terror from God spread over the people in all the towns of that area, so no one attacked Jacob's family.[6]Eventually, Jacob and his household arrived at Luz (also called Bethel) in Canaan."*

There was a singular purpose for which God was asking Jacob to return to Bethel –it was to enable him (Jacob) fulfil the vows he made years earlier. A covenant-keeping God does not forget the vows we make!

Realizing that he won't reach that goal, with all that He had seen and observed in his own household, Jacob asked them to surrender all their pagan idols, and purify themselves, as part of the preparations for the journey. What we are concerned with in this story as it relates to building to last is the fact that in spite of Jacob's personal devotion, building of altars – an equivalence of establishing many churches or building large auditoriums, a lot of idolatry was going on under his nose – right in the mission house (so to say)! This is part of the challenges of leadership. Again, we need to refer to the quote by Tim Ferriss (stated above):

> *"I value self-discipline, but creating systems that make it next to impossible to misbehave is more reliable than self control"*

It is not enough for a leader to be good, and upright, he must ensure that a system is in place that makes it almost impossible to misbehave! Institutionalized misbehaviour is perhaps one of the banes of today's church leadership, especially in Africa.

# THE SUCCESSFUL LEADER

It has often been said that 'success without a successor is failure'. That may not always be totally correct.

God is sovereign, and He is the One who chooses leaders as well as their successors - from Moses, Joshua, Eli, Samuel, Saul, David, Solomon, etc, to Elijah, Elisha, Paul, Timothy, etc.

In His sovereignty, He may choose or reveal successors to some leaders, and may not, to others. It is not a sign of strength or weakness on the part of the current or outgoing leaders.

Ordinarily, it will be expected that if, and since God revealed, as well as helped a leader to be chosen by his predecessor, he too will or should see the need to have a clear leader succeed him or her.

The Question or concern of some people as they go through the Bible, is: Why didn't Joshua appoint or have a clear successor to take over from him just as Moses did for Joshua? Many people have even taken it as a weakness or a short coming on Joshua's part. A look through the Scriptures show that it was not Joshua alone who did not bring forth a clear successor. Elisha, Timothy, Titus, etc did not, or could not. It may not necessarily be because Joshua (and all of these leaders), did not believe in succession

**Among several factors or reasons, this can be because:**
God may not have made it an essential part of their assignment or responsibilities. Also, Joshua (and some of these leaders) may have been pre-occupied with fulfilling the very calling and vision God gave them, that they did not make the issue of getting or appointing a clear Successor, their own business. It is also possible that they may have thought or believed that God - the owner of the Business, will sort such matters out in His infinite wisdom and at an appropriate time.
- Furthermore, (and this is where the sovereignty of God comes in again), HE knows that generations and their needs differ one from another. The assignments and

demands of leaders in different generations are also different. For example, there is a generation that rallies round a new leader, while another generation kills their emerging leaders even before such leaders ever step in!

What are all these saying to us? It is that we should:
- ** Stop blaming, criticizing, or even challenging a current or reigning leader to resign, retire, or compulsorily give us a successor.
- ** Also, we are to be sensitive to God's programme and agenda for each generation.
- ** In addition, we should thank God for what He has laid in the heart of our leaders and cooperate with them to fulfill such things.
- ** More importantly, we are to keep on praying that:
- \+ God should not put in the heart of a leader, anything that will not make the story of HIS Church complete.
- \+ No man will also push a leader into doing such things.
- \+ Finally, we are to do our best where God has put us, so as to lessen the burden of leadership.

Perhaps it could be pondered upon, the many likely outcomes, "IF JOSHUA HAD CHOSEN OR ANNOUNCED A CLEAR SUCCESSOR!

Such a man might have been frustrated out of the system, or outrightly murdered (physically, spiritually, character-wise, etc). Also, we may never have heard about great and courageous people like Deborah, Gideon, Jephthah, Samson, Eli, Samuel, and Kings like Saul, David, etc.

The truth is, many leaders are coming! They will emerge to complete the story of past and current leaders. They will emerge to take the Church to her promised land. They will emerge to take her to a state of perfection and readiness for the coming of our Lord and Saviour!

# THE SONS OF ELI

*"Now the sons of Eli were sons of Belial; they knew not the LORD ...18 But Samuel ministered before the LORD, being a child, girded with a linen ephod."*
**(I Samuel 2: 12, 18)**

The Scripture quoted above should be of great concern to all – both pastors, leaders, and parents alike.

The man Eli was both a priest, a husband, and a father. This calls for gratitude to God. This, for several reasons. First, it is not every man who is a husband. Many wish they are but are not. Also, not every husband is a father. Again, many wish they are but are yet to be. It is God alone who can make fruitful. I pray that all men who wish to be husbands of God-fearing and loving wives will be granted their hearts desires in due season in Jesus Name. We pray, in particular for Pastors and Ministers who may still be believing God for the fruit of the womb, may God visit them this season, as He did for Zechariah (the father of John the Baptist) in Jesus Name.

While the man Eli had every reason to be grateful to God that God made him a husband, a father, and a Minister of God, one should however be concerned for him that his sons did not get it right – both in life and ministry!

This brings us the realities of the challenge of balancing Ministry and family. As Ministers, we must ask God for wisdom to balance both, so that one does not suffer at the expense of the other. The Bible here called the sons of Eli, 'the sons of Belial!'

It is a basic truth that every child that is born into this world has a father – they are the children and sons of someone – a father. Whether the father owns up or accepts the responsibility of fatherhood is another thing entirely. Still talking about fathers, there are physical and spiritual fathers. Some fathers are also fathers by adoption, fathers by leadership, fathers in ministry, etc. More than all these, there is the Heavenly Father – He is superior, bigger, higher, and greater than all other fathers. He is not limited by what limits every other earthly father, whether biological or spiritual.

To understand the depravity of the sons of Eli, one may ask a few questions:
- Who is Belial, or what does it represent, a man, or a spirit?
- Who is a son of Belial? What are the marks or behavioural traits to look for in such a being?
- How and when did the sons of Eli turn to become sons of another father – this time, - Belial?

'Belial' is a biblical name of the devil or one of the fiends. It also means 'worthlessness'. (a 'Fiend' refers to an evil spirit or a demon. A 'Fiend' is also a very evil or cruel person).

From the above dictionary definition, Belial is a spirit - a negative and rebellious spirit - rebellious against God and His divine order. Belial is therefore a destructive spirit.

In our world today, and especially among the youths, and young Ministers, one can see the Belial and his human and institutional agents at work. When he possesses or takes over a man's life, he or she can hardly restrain him or herself from doing his bidding.

It is therefore obvious that all the evils and audacious atrocities done by Eli's sons were propelled by the spirit of Belial that had taken them over.

**Some even bigger questions then also arise. For instance,**

+ how and when did this evil transformation or derailing happen, and which particular doors did they open for the Belial spirit to come in?
+ which companies were the Sons of Eli keeping –both in and out of church - both physically and technologically? (Psalm 1:1-3) Were their parents – Priest and Mrs Eli aware of these 'friends?' (I Corinthians 15:33)
+ who and where was their mother – Mummy/Mrs Eli? If Pa Eli was very/too busy with Ministry work, what did she (Mrs Eli) do to help raise the sons?
+ Since the Bible was silent about Eli's wife, could it be that she died early and Eli the Priest was a single parent?
+ Also, was it a possibility that Mrs Eli was a thorn in his flesh - a nagging, incorrigible, husband-abuser, etc, kind of a wife and mother?

Finally, what was her own upbringing and bloodline like? Still on these sons with a double fatherhood, Vs 12 used the tense <u>'were'</u> in the phrase "were sons of Belial'-indicating that these boys or sons were not originally evil, but something happened to them along the line–as they grew up in life and ministry, and they turned to be or became something else. If this was so, I believe it could not have happened over night, it must have taken some time.

The Bible added that they 'knew not the Lord', this implies that they did not know the God of their father. They were not saved, yet, they became Ministers of God!

There are a couple of lessons to take from here: As Pastors and fathers, we should not assume that because we are Pastors, then our children are automatically saved. Never! That we are Pastors does not mean that our children are automatically saved. They, like every other child or youth and young adults must be led to personal conversion to Jesus.

Also, our children may not ordinarily and personally know, love, or even be interested in the God we are serving. They may not love, fear, trust, and want to serve our God. It is our important duty to pray and reach them for God.

The marks of those who do not know God are obvious (Daniel 11:32; Jeremiah 9:23-24):

> "[32] *Those who do wickedly against the covenant he shall* [a]*corrupt with flattery; but the people who know their God shall be strong, and carry out great exploits....*[23] *Thus says the* LORD: *"Let not the*

*wise man glory in his wisdom, Let not the mighty man glory in his might, Nor let the rich man glory in his riches;*[24]*But let him who glories glory in this, That he understands and knows Me, That I am the LORD, exercising loving kindness, judgment, and righteousness in the earth. For in these I delight," says the LORD."*

How then can we (and especially our children) know God? –The Bible, God's Word introduces Him, and tells us all that we need to know about Him.

The truth is that many of our (Pastors') children have a lot of CONFLICTS and QUESTIONS about GOD, even our God. Some of these conflicts and questions arise from the hypocrisy of we, their parents, and also that of other church leaders they see and watch: Other sources of such conflicts and questions are the evils of their generation and end time; the consequences of sin (and not from a wicked God, as some of them have been wrongly indoctrinated by today's humanistic and liberalistic agenda!) This great and holy God has rules and laws, and those who flout His laws cannot go scot free (just like anyone who breaks traffic laws should not expect to, but gets a fine or demerit, etc).

Even though God is a loving Father, who loves and forgives, yet, the offender must live with the consequences of his or her misdemeanours.

The Humanist agenda has one goal; it is to discredit God and His Word - the Bible. It in turn, seeks to confuse the minds of our children.

May I reiterate that GOD and HIS ETERNAL WORD ARE FOUNDATIONAL TO LIFE and PERSONAL PEACE. Man, his concepts, philosophies, science, discoveries theories, etc, are secondary and subject to God and His written Word.

How then can God help us to recover our children, Teens and youths from the deception of our age? It is by telling our children to believe the Bible and also weigh everything they see and hear, by the word of God; The Holy Bible (Psalm 119:128; Isa 40:8):

*"Therefore all Your precepts concerning all things I consider to be right; I hate every false way....The grass withers, the flower fades, But the word of our God stands forever."*

We are to also teach them never to consent to evil (which is often packaged as good in order to attract, entice, tempt, and lure them to destruction - Proverbs 1:10).

**Let us look at a brighter side of the story. This is in Verse 18 of our main Text:**

> *"But Samuel ministered before the LORD, being (as) a child, girded with a linen ephod."*

Samuel was different from Eli's sons - he knew, he saw, and he heard all the evil deeds of the 'Big Boys'. However, while Eli's sons were turning to sons of Belial, Samuel was gradually growing and turning to a great man of God – a national Prophet. He did not join others to do evil (Psalm 1:1-3):

> *"Oh, the joys of those who do not follow the advice of the wicked, or stand around with sinners, or join in with mockers. But they delight in the law of the LORD, meditating on it day and night. They are like trees planted along the riverbank, bearing fruit each season. Their leaves never wither, and they prosper in all they do."*

Your own children, and mine can be different! While other children are rotting and wasting away, our own children can know, love and fear God. They can excel in life and do great exploits in various spheres and endeavours. They can also be ministering to God and become Ministers of God. They can be a blessing to their generation.

May God help us to raise our children for Him in Jesus Name.

There seem to be a great trouble, calamity, and disaster looming in the Church or God's House nowadays. It might be mainly due to the many sons of Belial that are in (or had taken over) the Pulpit as Priest, Pastors, Ministers, and even Bishops or General Overseers! (See I Samuel 2 Vs 12-17, 22). Who they are, what they did, and are doing -just all that the sons of Eli did, or even more!

The effect on the Church, on Christianity, and on the society could best be imagined.

Will God be silent and overlook it for ever? The answer is NEVER! He will do what He did before (unto the sons of Eli). He can de-robe them, He can take ministry away from their family line, and He can ultimately KILL them!

God is a God who is rich in mercy. As many of them who are willing to genuinely repent and be purged, God will restore to the altar and bring back to His true and holy place of worship. He will also restore His presence and power. The time to repent is NOW!

# "IN THE DAYS OF SAMUEL"

*"...And the hand of the Lord was against the Philistines all the Days of Samuel."*
- I Samuel 7:13c

Samuel was a widely known name in the Bible. Several things made him popular. These include the circumstances of his birth, the values he lived by, some historical events that characterized his Ministry, as well as the legacy he left behind at the end of his Ministry and life.

Samuel was a covenant child. Born by Hannah, a woman who had been barren for years.

In fulfilment of her vow, Samuel was taken by his mother at a very tender age to go and be living in the Temple at Shiloh. Samuel did not just grow up in a Christian home or temple, he grew up in God's house and presence - It was not Eli or his wife that nursed and raised Samuel, it was God Himself! Hence his life was different from Eli's children. Samuel's life, his days, his words were all God's. No wonder God too backed him up and brought lasting results.

Samuel grew up before the Lord, and started hearing and recognizing God's voice as a young boy. Even though there were 'bad' boys around him even in the priest's house, one way or the other, God kept Samuel uncontaminated. God later used him to anoint the first two Kings for Israel in the persons of Saul (the son of Kish the Benjaminite), and David (the son of Jesse). When Israel demanded an earthly King from God, Samuel was unhappy, but God asked him to yield to their request.

As a man of unquestionable integrity, Samuel openly challenged the whole Nation; asking anyone who has a single evidence, to come out, and point out if he owed them something. Hear him in In I Samuel 12:1-5:

> *"Then Samuel addressed all Israel: "I have done as you asked and given you a king. 2 Your king is now your leader. I stand here before you—an old, gray-haired man—and my sons serve you. I have served as*

*your leader from the time I was a boy to this very day. 3 Now testify against me in the presence of the Lord and before his anointed one. Whose ox or donkey have I stolen? Have I ever cheated any of you? Have I ever oppressed you? Have I ever taken a bribe and perverted justice? Tell me and I will make right whatever I have done wrong." 4 "No," they replied, "you have never cheated or oppressed us, and you have never taken even a single bribe." 5 "The Lord and his anointed one are my witnesses today," Samuel declared, "that my hands are clean." (NLT)*

Our opening Text referred to "The Days of Samuel".

By "The Days of Samuel", the Bible was talking about the tenure of Samuel as a prophet and judge in, and over Israel. How long, and what were the highlights and unique things that happened in the days of Samuel?:

Among the several special things that happened during the tenure of Samuel as Prophet in Israel, three stood out:
- The restoration of the Nation back to God (I Samuel 7:7-14);
- The appointment (and later the removal) of Saul - the first king in Israel (I Samuel 10:1; I Samuel 15:1).
- The anointing of David as the second king of Israel (I Samuel 16: 7-13).

Let us look at the three events a little more closely.

## The restoration of the Nation back to God:
In I Samuel 7:7-14, we read:
> *"Now when the Philistines heard that the children of Israel had gathered together at Mizpah, the lords of the Philistines went up against Israel. And when the children of Israel heard of it, they were afraid of the Philistines. So the children of Israel said to Samuel, "Do not cease to cry out to the Lord our God for us, that He may save us from the hand of the Philistines." And Samuel took a suckling lamb and offered it as a whole burnt offering to the Lord. Then Samuel cried out to the Lord for Israel, and the Lord answered him. Now as Samuel was offering up the burnt offering, the Philistines drew near to battle against Israel. But the Lord thundered with a loud thunder upon the Philistines that day, and so confused them that they were overcome before Israel. And the men of Israel went out of Mizpah and pursued the Philistines, and drove them back as far as below Beth Car. Then Samuel took a stone and set it up between Mizpah and Shen, and called its name Ebenezer, saying, "Thus far the Lord has helped us." So the Philistines were subdued, and they did not come anymore into the territory of Israel. And the*

> *hand of the Lord was against the Philistines all the days of Samuel. Then the cities which the Philistines had taken from Israel were restored to Israel, from Ekron to Gath; and Israel recovered its territory from the hands of the Philistines. Also there was peace between Israel and the Amorites. And Samuel judged Israel all the days of his life."*

In the above Text, we see how God used Samuel to restore Israel back to Himself. Here, Samuel called a Solemn Assembly or National repentance, and challenged the whole Nation to put away their idols – all that had stolen their hearts from God - the physical objects that had become gods, as well as the idols in their hearts. Israel heeded Samuel's call, and while the Service was still going on, the Philistines - Israel's arch enemy, came as they had done several times in the past. However, this time they miscalculated! They did not know that the equation of Israel's relationship with God had changed, and that God had returned to His people. The Bible recorded that

> *"the Lord thundered with a loud thunder upon the Philistines that day, and so confused them that they were overcome before Israel. And the men of Israel went out of Mizpah and pursued the Philistines, and drove them back as far as below Beth Car."*

Dear Reader, do you have a personal relationship with God through His Son the Lord Jesus? If not, you can, right now. All you need is to humbly acknowledge that you are a sinner who deserves God's wrath and judgment. Then thank God for sending Jesus who already took your place on the Cross. Ask

God for mercy and forgiveness. Finally, ask Jesus to wash you clean with His Blood from all your sins. Then invite Him into your heart as your personal Saviour, Lord, and King. (Please see Rom 13:23; Roman 6:23; Acts 4:12; Romans 10:9-13; Isaiah 55:6-7; I John 1:5-9; II Corinthians 5:17-21).

Perhaps you once knew God, but your relationship had gone sour because you allowed some idols to become gods in your life, Jesus can restore you. The equation of your relationship can change for the better. Thereafter, God will step in, into your situation, and all who had been mocking you - asking where is your God will now want to serve your God.

To end that day, the Bible said "Then Samuel took a stone and set it up between Mizpah and Shen, and called its name Ebenezer, saying, "Thus far the Lord has helped us."

Has God ever helped you before? If your answer is Yes, I have a good news for you. God will help you again! He has not changed. He has not lost any of His power. Today God will help you. He will help your children. God will help me too.

**-The appointment (and later the removal), of Saul - the first king in Israel (I Samuel 10:1; I Samuel 15:1):**

The appointment of Saul as the first king was a great milestone in the history of Israel as a Nation. Even though God, the Almighty had always been King over His chosen people, meeting all their needs, and also fighting their battles, yet they still demanded for a physical king – the one they could see, and someone who would go before them whenever they went to fight!

At first, Samuel was not happy about the request but God asked him to go ahead and give them a king. God even revealed Saul to the Prophet, and he did anoint Saul as king. However, that was a permissive will of God. And, like every permissive will always bring an immediate or short term euphoria or satisfaction of having our own way, the Israelites, oblivious of the future, were glad that they now had a king - 'the man of the people!'

This is why, in relation to our subject matter – "In the days of Samuel", the rejection of Saul as king appears more significant than even his appointment as the first king in Israel.

A critical Question that had crossed many minds is "Couldn't God have forgiven the disobedience of king Saul – especially the way he handled the instructions God gave him in the matter of the Amalekites?" I believe HE could have. Perhaps, however, HE did not because not only did Saul disobey God's clear instructions to him through Prophet Samuel, Saul went far beyond that! He, Saul, insisted that in the matter of the Amalekites, he did exactly what God asked him to. Integrity is at stake here – Samuel, and God's. Since Samuel knew he delivered God's message as accurately as possible and God – the all knowing knew too that Samuel neither added or subtracted from the message HE gave him for king Saul, it became clear that Saul was indirectly trying to give God a name HE does not bear - making God a liar (Numbers 23:19; Hebrews 6:18; Romans 3:4). A vivid look at Saul's statement (see and compare verses 2-3, 7-9, 14-16, 18-21), show clearly Saul's mind.

In verses 22-25 Samuel bared Gods mind further:

*"So Samuel said: "Has the Lord as great delight in burnt offerings and sacrifices, As in obeying the voice of the Lord? Behold, to obey is better than sacrifice, And to heed than the fat of rams. For rebellion is as the sin of witchcraft, And stubbornness is as iniquity and idolatry. Because you have rejected the word of the Lord, He also has rejected you from being king." Then Saul said to Samuel, "I have sinned, for I have*

*transgressed the commandment of the Lord and your words, because I feared the people and obeyed their voice. Now therefore, please pardon my sin, and return with me, that I may worship the Lord."*

*On hearing this, Saul with his own mouth said, "I have sinned against God." Yet, he was asking forgiveness from man! He told Prophet Samuel "Please forgive me and honour me before the people."*

When God has rejected a man, a king, or a leader, but rather than such a man resorting to the closet to make things right with God, if he continues to seek the honour of men, anyone who still continues to worship with, or under him might be in great danger – the danger of an unequal yoke! Hence Samuel refused to go and worship with Saul.

Samuel's concern about Israel's request for a king had a lesser effect than the consequences of a king rejected by God. When a leader – be it the leader of a family, an organisation, a political, a royal, a spiritual leader is rejected by God, it speaks volume. No wonder Samuel mourned unendingly for Saul until God jolted him back into reality that life must continue and that HIS people Israel could not continue without a new leader. Hence, in 1Samuel 16: 1, we read:

*"Now the Lord said to Samuel, "How long will you mourn for Saul, seeing I have rejected him from*

*reigning over Israel? Fill your horn with oil, and go; I am sending you to Jesse the Bethlehemite. For I have provided Myself a king among his sons."*

Even though already rejected, God still kept Saul in the palace, but definitely not on the throne any more!

## The anointing of David as the second king of Israel (I Samuel 16: 7-13).

Another significant event in the days of Samuel was the anointing of David as the second king over Israel.

In 1Samuel 16: 7-13, we read:

[7]   *But the Lord said to Samuel, "Do not look at his appearance or at his physical stature, because I have refused him. For the Lord does not see as man sees; for man looks at the outward appearance, but the Lord looks at the heart."*

[8]   *So Jesse called Abinadab, and made him pass before Samuel. And he said, "Neither has the Lord chosen this one."*

[9]   *Then Jesse made Shammah pass by. And he said, "Neither has the Lord chosen this one."*

[10]  *Thus Jesse made seven of his sons pass before Samuel. And Samuel said to Jesse, "The Lord has not chosen these."*

[11]   *And Samuel said to Jesse, "Are all the young men here?" Then he said, "There remains yet the youngest, and there he is, keeping the sheep." And Samuel said to Jesse, "Send and bring him. For we will not sit down till he comes here."*

[12]   *So he sent and brought him in. Now he was ruddy, with bright eyes, and good-looking. And the Lord said, "Arise, anoint him; for this is the one!" [13]Then Samuel took the horn of oil and anointed him in the midst of his brothers; and the Spirit of the Lord came upon David from that day forward. So Samuel arose and went to Ramah. A Distressing Spirit Troubles Saul.*

After God has allayed the fear of Prophet Samuel that Saul could in desperation harm him if, and whenever he heard that a new king had been installed while he was still alive, he Samuel arrived at Jesse's house. On this particular day, the Shepherd boy David, woke up as on any other day before and went on his normal business. Then about mid-afternoon he got a call from home to come over. On getting home he saw everybody standing including his father, Jesse. He must have wondered 'what's going on here?' Then suddenly, someone started pouring oil upon his head, and then proclaimed him the next king of Israel. To David it must have appeared like a dream!

All said, in relation to the issues of leadership succession, and building to last, 'The Days of Samuel and some of the major events associated with it teach us one thing: every leader must work towards leaving behind a positive legacy – he or she must strive to be a monumental person – one who is remembered for righteousness, faithfulness, and the fear of God. May God help us all in Jesus Name.

# CATCHING THE SPIRIT OF THE LEADER (FINISHING WELL)

Apostle Paul, among other things, in Philipians 4:9, made some statements:

*"The things which ye both learned and received and heard and saw in me, these things do: and the God of peace shall be with you."*

He had earlier in this same Epistle (Philipians 3:17-18), lamented thus:

*"Brethren, be ye imitators together of me, and mark them that so walk even as ye have us for an ensample. For many walk, of whom I told you often, and now*

*tell you even weeping, that they are the enemies of the cross of Christ"*

Apostle Paul seem to be comparing two sets of people here. The first set are those who walked as he walked. He admonished that he, and such people should be imitated, or made a role model. This is a true and Biblical discipleship that makes it possible to 'build to last'. Second, are those (and they seem to be more in number), who operate as enemies of the cross! Apostle Paul was not talking about a Terrorist group here, or some religious fundamentalists, rather, he was talking about Christian workers, ministers, and probably pastors!

As in normal situations, when you grow up within a system/or environment, you spend some considerable time under different leaders. As you do so, you acquire their nature or behavioural patterns, and, <u>consciously</u> or <u>unconsciously</u>, you begin to act out some of them. I call it '<u>catching the spirit of the leader</u>'.

Thus, in Philipians 4:9, Apostle Paul went on and said:
> *"The things which ye both learned and received and heard and saw in me, these things do: and the God of peace shall be with you."*

This means that every man has a choice who to pattern his life and ministry after. Whether those who say and do the right things, or those who say and do the wrong things.

It appears that rather than pattern their lives and ministries (and probably their families), after God-fearing pastors and leaders, many have chosen to pattern their lives and ministries after those who say and do the wrong things! This is perhaps one of the greatest challenges that many Mission-sending churches are facing globally today. The rat race for position, influence, and affluence seem to be at a serious degree.

Already, it seems some of the upcoming youths have already been caught up in the web, and there is an urgent need for help! (Please see Matthew 6:4-6; Acts 10:34-35; Hebrews 19; Revelation 22:10-12).

Dear Reader, perhaps among other things, your prayers henceforth should include:
+ Father, any person or leader that I have passed through or that had passed through me, who has deposited anything evil in my life that is already affecting me negatively, this morning send Your fire to destroy all their evil deposits.
+ Father, everywhere I have led wrongly and misled your people, Father, please forgive me.

- Father, any person or leader that I have passed through or that had passed through me, who has deposited anything evil in my life that is already affecting me negatively, please send Your fire to destroy all their evil deposits.
- Father, please help me to love/hate what You love/hate. Help me to be like JESUS.
- Father, both in secret and in the open, help me to do what is right in Your eyes.
- Father, when You come to do the Final marking, please don't let me be found wanting.

# Acknowledgments

I thank God for inspiring this book that you have in your hand. I thank all the Brethren and friends who have continued to lift up our hands, and encouraged us in the work that God has called us to do, especially in this part of the world. They include John and Esther Adegboye, Femi and Faith Odumade, Abiodun Doherty, Tunde and Kemi Fadahunsi, Wale and Bukky Omolokun, Kolapo and Kenny Adigun, Niyi Borire, Olaitan and Funmi Oyefeso, Stella and Akin Oyemade, Omowunmi and Isaac Adewunmi, Mary and Sam Olaniyan, and many others. I wish to also specially thank Enoch Alimi who did the cover design, as well as Mrs Funmi Agbi and Tunde Ajeyomi who took time to painstakingly go through the manuscript.

May the Lord continue to make all your affairs to run smoothly, and ensure you flourish in all you do in Jesus Name.

Finally, I thank my immediate family for all their love, prayers and endurance. It shall never be in vain in Jesus Name.

Abraham Haastrup,
Melbourne, Australia.
August, 2021

# Appendices

SHAPE - (Discovering Your Fit in the Body of Christ)
1. The real truth: - You are shaped for significance - to make you become a person of destiny.

**Note:**
+ Everything in life & Creation has a shape. You too have a shape!
+ God - your Creator shaped you for significance.
+ You need to discover your Shape so that you can become significant, & also become a person of destiny.
+ There are <u>five Keys</u> to Discovering your true Shape:
- Spiritual gift
- Heart (what God has put in your heart to do - your passion)

- Abilities (Develop & deploy, or lose them)!
- Personality
- Experiences
* These Keys are received through LIFE & SOAP.

LIFE - (Listen, Inquire, Faith, Experience)
SOAP - (Scriptures, Observation, Application, Prayer) Note: LIFE + SOAP = SHAPE

**The ultimate purpose** of LIFE & SOAP is to help you discover your SHAPE so that you can become significant, & also become a person of destiny.

**Notes:**
1. **Bill Lawrence** (President of Leader Formation International, Bible.org
2. The writer of **"Empty Truth"** – (material was said to have been written by **Mark Klages** – *a former US Marine & a lifelong Teacher who focuses n applying a Cnristian Worldview to everyday events*)
3. **Bishop Oyedepo, David** – in 'Wisdom for Better Approach"
4. The concepts of '**LIFE**', '**SOAP**', & '**SHAPE**' were first brought to my attention by an Elderly Christian, **Rod Denton** (of Equipping the Next Generation) based in Adelaide, South Australia.

5. **Nuzzi Gianluigi** - *Merchants in the Temple (Inside Pope Francis's Secret Battle Against Corruption In the Vatican), Pages 68.*
6. As the name suggests, 'Guidelines' are like boundary lines outside which a runner must not go. He or she is however free to maneuver, even if to his or her advantages, and to the disadvantages of the organization. On the other hand, 'Manuals' are step-by-step operational tools that state in unambiguous ways, the procedure and processes that must be followed by all in the day to day activities of the entity or organization.
7. **Tim Ferriss** – as quoted by **Olugbemi Bayo** in "When Tomorrow Comes" (EventsConnect Ltd., Lagos, Nigeria 2014).

# For Further Reading:

- **Fomum, Zacharias Tanee**- *The Leader & His God*, (Editions du livre Chretien, France, 2015).
- **Maxwell, John**-*21 Irrefutable Laws of Leadership* (Thomas Nelson, 1998).

**Atteberry, Mark** - *The Solomon Seduction: What You Can Learn From The Wisest Fool In The Bible*– (W Publishing Group, 2014).

**Graham, Billy** - *Nearing Home* (W Publishing Group, 2011).

**Spurgeon, Charles** - *Holy Spirit Power* (Whitaker House, 1996).

**Akanni, Gbile** - *Our Mission in the World (2018 MLR - Issue Paper)*
Thomas Macaulay (1800-1859) - British writer and politician,

**Max Lucado** - *God will Use This for Good*(Thomas Nelson,Nashville, Tennessee, 2013).

**Max Lucado** - *Live to Make a Difference*- (Thomas Nelson,Nashville, Tennessee, 2010).

**Addison Steve**- *The Rise and Fall of Movements* - 100 Movements Publishing, 2019).

**Kotter, John**- *Our Iceberg Is Melting!*(Changing & Succeeding Under Any Conditions)

**Adeboye, E.A**- "*Open Heavens*" is a popular daily devotional guide written and published by Pastor E.A. Adeboye (General Overseer of TRCCG). "<u>*Empty Truth*</u>" appeared on 04/02/19.

**Adeboye, E.A -** "*Open Heavens*": Watch Your Words At All Times I (01/07/2020).

**Olukoya, DK -** *Personal Spiritual Check up* (MFM Ministries, Lagos, Nigeria, 1996).

Canfield, Jack, etc (Mark V Hansen+Les Hewitt) - *The Power of Focus* (Health Communications Inc, Deerfield, Florida, 2000).

**Wurmbrand, Richard-** *Alone with God* (Living Sacrifice Books,1999).

**Nuzzi Gianluigi-** *Merchants in the Temple (Inside Pope Francis's Secret Battle Against Corruption In the Vatican)*,Henry Holt & Co, 2015.

**<u>Haastrup, Abraha:</u>**
- *The Christian Worker* (Sunrise Foundation International, 2014).
- *The First Voice* - (Sunrise Foundation International, 2017).

**Olugbemi Bayo** in "When Tomorrow Comes" (EventsConnect Ltd., Lagos, Nigeria 2014).

www.ingramcontent.com/pod-product-compliance
Lightning Source LLC
Chambersburg PA
CBHW070614010526
44118CB00012B/1516